Illustrator
Phil Hopkins

Editor
Mary Kaye Taggart

Editorial Project Manager
Karen J. Goldfluss, M.S. Ed.

Editor-in-Chief
Sharon Coan, M.S. Ed.

Art Director
Elayne Roberts

Associate Designer
Denise Bauer

Cover Artist
Chris Macabitas

Product Manager
Phil Garcia

Imaging
Ralph Olmedo, Jr.

Publishers
Rachelle Cracchiolo, M.S. Ed.
Mary Dupuy Smith, M.S. Ed.

Conflict RESOLUTION

GRADES 5-8

Author

Julia Jasmine, M.A.

Teacher Created Materials, Inc.
6421 Industry Way
Westminster, CA 92683
www.teachercreated.com
©1997 Teacher Created Materials, Inc.
Reprinted, 2001
Made in U.S.A.
ISBN-1-57690-104-1

Table of Contents

Introduction

Conflict Resolution is more than just a book of techniques for resolving conflicts. It is, first and foremost, a systematic program designed to show teachers methods that will help their students to ward off or even bypass many conflicts altogether. It also presents nonviolent ways (assertiveness, negotiation, compromise, and mediation) to resolve the conflicts that do occur.

This program will take teachers and their students (grade levels 5–8) through the steps of developing healthy self-concepts, growing in social awareness, acquiring communication skills, and developing respect and empathy for others. Students will be encouraged to consider the relationships among these important concepts: competition and cooperation, rules and self-direction, equal treatment and special circumstances, justice and compassion. Finally, students will be given information about and practice in using techniques for conflict resolution. A bonus thematic unit about peace is also included.

How to Use This Book

The first four sections of *Conflict Resolution* are organized by grade level. The topics and subtopics are the same at each grade level, but the lessons under these topics and subtopics are different and age appropriate. Depending on the group of students you are teaching (consider their age, maturity, and experience) you can choose activities from any of the grade levels to suit your needs.

The first topic at each grade level is **Who Am I? Developing Self-Concepts**. Most experts in child growth and development (educators, as well as psychologists) agree that growth in self-concept, including self-esteem, is a basic step in getting along with others. If young people, or adults for that matter, do not see themselves as separate and valuable, they cannot see others as separate and valuable either. In the Who Am I? sections, students will be given the opportunity to get to know themselves better.

The second topic at each grade level, **Who Are You? Growing in Social Awareness**, directs the students' attention outward to focus on others. Pre-adolescents and adolescents, who may already be very social, often need help in directing their social skills in constructive ways. In the Who Are You? sections, students will be given opportunities to get to know each other.

The third topic, **Can We Talk? Acquiring Communication Skills**, deals with an area that is often taken for granted. Just because people can talk does not mean that they are able to communicate! Students can be taught the basics of communication, thus increasing their ability to understand one another.

The fourth topic, **Why Should We Care? Developing Respect and Empathy**, uses literature to help students recognize the fact that everyone has the right to his or her own opinions and that everyone feels the same emotions.

The remaining topics are directed at all four grade levels. The section entitled **Are We Making Progress? Age-Appropriate Concerns** deals with issues that students in this age group tend to feel strongly about: the importance of competition, the necessity for rules, the value of equal treatment, and the significance of justice. Although there is certainly nothing wrong with these standards for behavior, it is important that students also recognize the relevance of cooperation, self-direction, special circumstances, and compassion. This section will give the students an opportunity to compare these qualities and determine when one is more appropriate than another in a given situation.

The last topic, **Can We Get Along? Using Techniques for Conflict Resolution**, gives students some real tools to use in dealing with disagreements, from the smallest argument to the most potentially dangerous dispute.

At the end of the book you will find a **Bonus Section** consisting of **A Thematic Unit About Peace**. It could be equally effective used as an orientation for the activities in this book or, at the end, as a culmination and celebration of what your students have learned.

Fifth Grade

Developing Self-Concepts

My Name: Nicknames

Purpose:

to give students the opportunity to select nicknames which suit their personalities

Materials:

- ◆ stacks of old sports magazines
- ◆ half-sheets of construction paper
- ◆ scissors and glue sticks
- ◆ copies of the writing prompt on page 7, one for each student
- ◆ pens or pencils

Activity—Part 1:

Tell the students . . . Athletes very often have great nicknames. Look through some magazines and find sports figures who have nicknames. Each of you is going to be making your own collage by cutting out pictures of your favorite athlete and gluing them onto a piece of construction paper. Then, cut out large, fancy letters that spell your athlete's nickname and add them to your collage.

Display the finished products on a sports bulletin board entitled "Sports Nicknames."

Activity—Part 2:

Ask the students . . . Have you ever wished you were a great athlete? An Olympic skater? An NBA basketball player? A champion swimmer? A professional football player? Think of having your picture on the cover of a sports magazine and under the picture would be your nickname! What would it be?

Pass out the writing prompt. Give your students ample time to think and write. If you use the writing process, this can be a "quick write" or a first draft. Then give the students the opportunity to later do the editing and revising steps.

When the papers are completed (for your purposes), ask for volunteers to read their pieces aloud to the group. Remind the audience of good listening manners and the necessity for making positive comments.

Evaluation and Processing:

Discuss the collages and nicknames of the sports figures. Do their nicknames fit their sports? (Slugger) The way they play their positions? (Boomer) Something about the way they look? (Slim) Or some personality characteristic? (Magic)

Discuss the nicknames chosen by the students for themselves. What special meanings do these nicknames have?

Developing Self-Concepts

My Name: Nicknames

Name_____ Date _____

Writing Situation:

Pretend you have suddenly become a famous athlete. What do people call you? What do they yell when you walk out onto the court or the field or when you dive into the pool or skate out on the ice?

Directions for Writing:

Write about your nickname as a famous athlete. Tell how you got it and why it suits you. Explain how you feel when you hear this nickname. Express your thoughts in complete sentences. If you need more space, continue writing on the back of this paper.

_____

_____

_____

_____

_____

_____

_____

_____

_____

_____

_____

_____

_____

Developing Self-Concepts

How I Look: My Favorite Outfit

Purpose:

to give students the opportunity to think about how they express themselves through the clothes they wear

Materials:

- ◆ copies of page 9, one for each student
- ◆ an enlarged copy of page 9 for the teacher
- ◆ pens or pencils
- ◆ crayons, markers, etc.

Activity—Part 1:

Tell the students . . . People often express the way they feel about themselves through the clothes they wear. We all have a favorite outfit—something that feels just right every time we wear it. We might say, "This outfit is really me!" Discuss.

Activity—Part 2:

Pass out copies of page 9 and demonstrate its use with your enlarged copy. You can sketch an outfit on the stick figure, color it in, and add labels with arrows. (See below.) No one will need to be an artist to complete this activity.

When the sketches are complete, meet in a large group to share them. Be sure to ask the students to comment on why they chose the outfits they sketched.

Evaluation and Processing:

Discuss the activity . . . Why are clothes so important to people? What do your clothes say about you? Why do people tend to like one of their own outfits better than the others they have? Do you feel differently about clothes this year than you did last year?

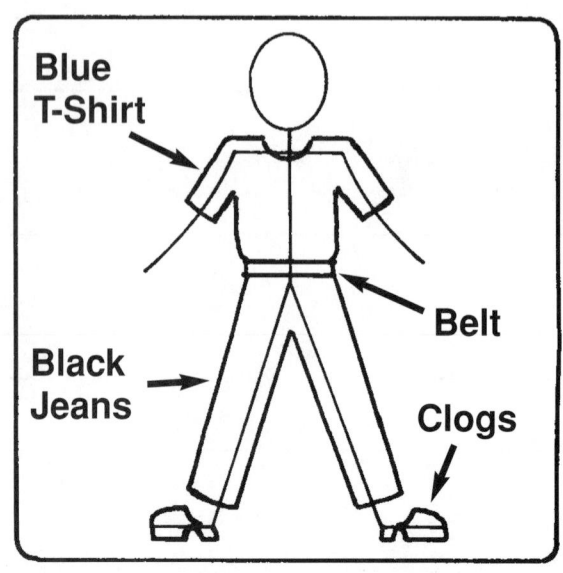

8

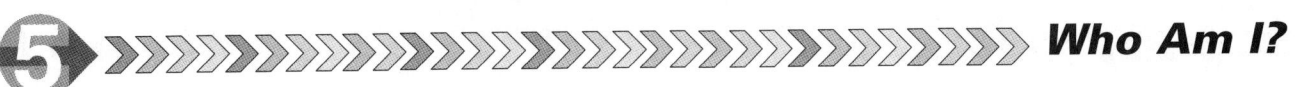

Developing Self-Concepts

How I Look: My Favorite Outfit

Directions: Sketch and then color one of your favorite outfits onto the stick figure below. Label the various parts of the outfit.

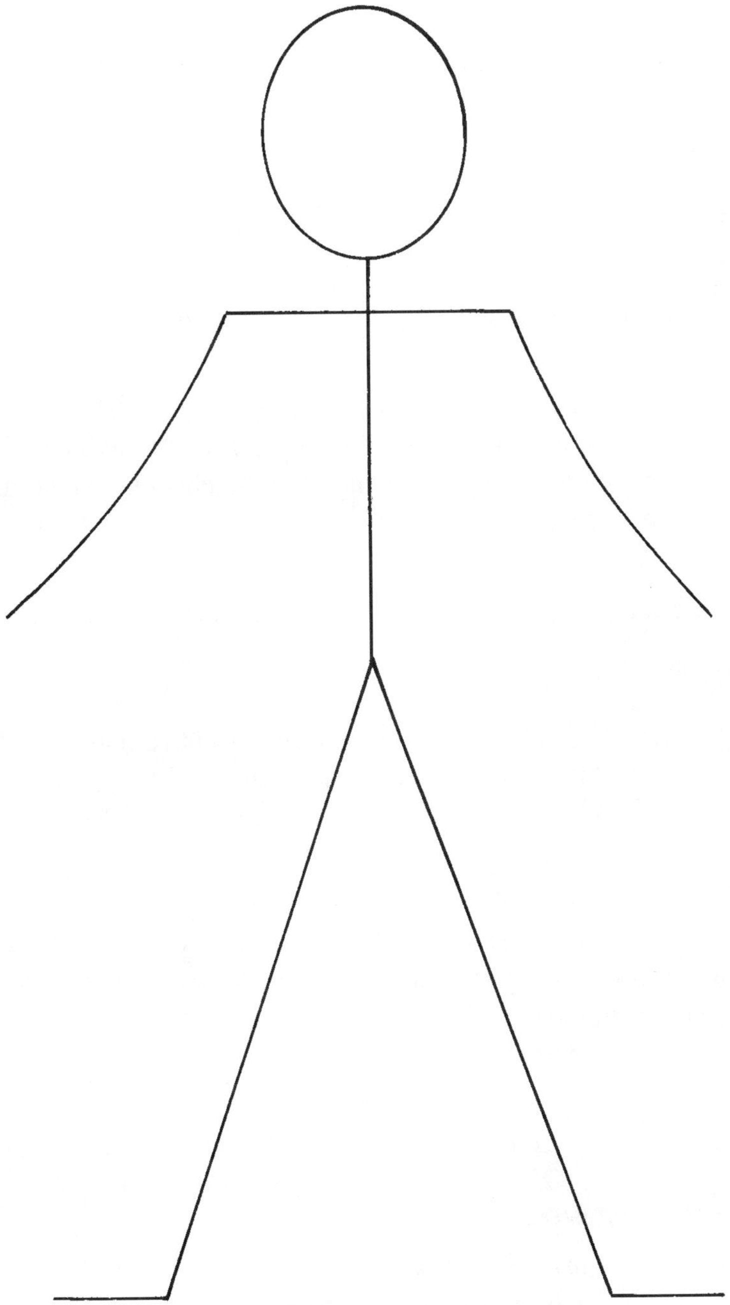

Developing Self-Concepts

What I Know: What I Can Do

Purpose:

to help students think about the things they already know how to do and the things that they can look forward to mastering based on grade-level expectations

Materials:

◆ copies of page 11, one for each student (or make up your own checklist based on your own school or district skill lists)

◆ red and blue markers or crayons

Activity—Part 1:

Begin this activity with the entire class. Show your students the checklist and its boxes. Discuss the things they already know how to do and the things they can look forward to learning during the school year.

Pass out the checklists. Tell the students they will be marking only the boxes in the "Now" column at this time. Have them use a red marker (or crayon) to check off the things they already know and a blue one for things they are going to learn. Read each item from the checklist aloud and give the students time to decide if the item is something they already know how to do (red) or something they are going to learn (blue).

Collect the completed checklists and put them away for use in Part 2 of this activity.

Activity—Part 2:

You will know when to expect all of the students in your class to have mastered the checklist items on page 11. If anyone is having trouble with a particular skill, you can devote some time to that skill and that student before using the checklist for the second time. The idea, of course, is to have all of the students color all of the "Now" boxes red.

At the appropriate time, toward the end of the school year, pass out the checklists again. Then repeat the activity, reading the items aloud and having the students check off the boxes in the column labeled "Later." Walk around the room while this is being done to make sure that everyone is using red markers. If someone is considering using a blue marker, stop and ask why. If you feel that the student who is hesitating has mastered the skill, ask that student to demonstrate the skill in question for his or her own satisfaction.

Send the checklists home with the students or post them around the classroom for everyone to see.

Evaluation and Processing:

Encourage students to enjoy their successes. Ask the students: Which skills were the easiest? hardest? most fun? Which ones made them feel the proudest of themselves?

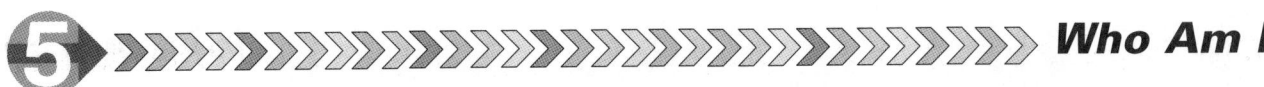

Developing Self-Concepts

What I Know: What I Can Do

Directions: Check off the items you know how to do with a red marker or crayon. Use a blue marker or crayon to check off the items you do not know how to do. Fill in only the "Now" column this time. You will fill in the "Later" column later in the year.

Skill	Now	Later
1. I can add, subtract, multiply, and divide whole numbers.	☐	☐
2. I can add, subtract, multiply, and divide decimals.	☐	☐
3. I can add, subtract, multiply, and divide fractions.	☐	☐
4. I can observe, record, and organize scientific data.	☐	☐
5. I can sequence the historical events I have studied.	☐	☐
6. I know the continents and can find places on a map.	☐	☐
7. I can read and understand grade level materials.	☐	☐
8. I can express my ideas orally and in writing.	☐	☐
9. I can use periods and capital letters.	☐	☐
10. I can spell many of the words I use in writing.	☐	☐
11. I know how to use a dictionary and encyclopedia.	☐	☐
12. I can work with others in a cooperative group.	☐	☐

Developing Self-Concepts

How I Feel: Too Young or Too Old

Purpose:

to help students deal with being "too young" for many things that they want to do and yet "too old" for many other things

Materials:

◆ copies of page 13, one for each student

◆ pens or pencils

Activity—Part 1:

Students in the fifth grade are at a difficult time for dealing with accurate and/or positive self-concepts. Many of the things they still like to do are considered babyish either by the adults they interact with, their peer group, or by the fifth grader himself or herself.

Ask the students to fill out the activity sheet on page 13 by listing some of these confusing messages.

Activity—Part 2:

Ask the students to volunteer to share their lists with the rest of the class. Do many students share the same experiences? How do they feel when they are told they are too old for something? (Embarrassed? Cheated?) How do they feel when they are told they are too young for something? (Disappointed? Let down?) Which things do they tell themselves they are too old or too young to have or to do? Are they making their own lives unnecessarily difficult? Maybe some things are all right no matter how young or how old a person is. (Teddy bears, for example, are loved by people of all ages. During World War II the Royal Air Force pilots of England used to take their teddy bears with them when they flew raids over Germany. Many older people still have teddy bears that they consider their friends. Doctors think that teddy bears are good for sick people and can help them to get well by making them feel more secure.)

Evaluation and Processing:

Discuss the activity . . . What can you do to make this time of your life easier and less frustrating? How could you help yourself feel better when you are told you are too old to do or have something? How could you help yourself feel better when you are told you are too young to do or have something?

Developing Self-Concepts

How I Feel: Too Young or Too Old

Name_____ Date _____

Directions: Finish the sentences below.

> I feel really grown up sometimes, but people say I am too young to . . .

- _____
- _____
- _____
- _____
- _____
- _____

> I feel like a little kid sometimes, but people say I am too old to . . .

- _____
- _____
- _____
- _____
- _____
- _____
- _____
- _____
- _____

Growing in Social Awareness

Names: I Know You

Purpose:

to give every student the opportunity to learn the names of all the other students in the class and to associate the names with the right people

Materials:

- ◆ mailboxes (cubbyholes, divided cardboard cartons, etc.) with name labels, one for each student

- ◆ copies of page 15, one for each student

- ◆ pens or pencils

Activity—Part 1:

This part of the activity can simply be part of your classroom management plan. Set up a daily routine during which one student stands at the mailboxes and calls off the names of the other students one at a time. When a student hears his or her name announced, he or she may walk up to the caller to get mail/papers. At that time the student calling the names will begin to associate the person who comes to get the papers with the name that was called. Rotate the caller assignment until everyone in the class has had at least one turn.

Activity—Part 2:

Tell the students . . . It is a known fact that we are more apt to get along with people if we know their names. They become real to us, and we realize that they are people too with the same feelings we have.

Pass out the writing prompt (page 15). Give your students ample time to think and write. If you use the writing process, this can be a "quick write" or a first draft. Then give the students the opportunity to later do the editing and revising steps.

When the papers are completed (for your purposes), ask for volunteers to read their pieces aloud to the group. Remind the audience of good listening manners and the necessity for making positive comments.

Evaluation and Processing:

Test your students on the names they know. Have a contest to see who can call the most people by their correct names. Discuss the advantages of knowing the names of everyone in the class. What are the benefits? Do you enjoy having other people call you by your name?

Growing in Social Awareness

Names: I Know You

Name_____ Date _____

Writing Situation:

We have been doing activities to help us learn each other's names. You may have learned the names of quite a few people whom you did not know by name before.

Directions for Writing:

Pick a person whose name you have recently learned. Do you feel differently about that person since you know him or her by name? Why? In what way? Express your thoughts in complete sentences. If you need more space, continue writing on the back of this paper.

_____

_____

_____

_____

_____

_____

_____

_____

_____

_____

_____

_____

_____

_____

Growing in Social Awareness

Qualities: I Like You Because . . .

Purpose:

to encourage students to become aware of and appreciate the good qualities of their classmates

Materials:

◆ copies of page 17, one for each student

◆ one enlarged copy of page 17 for the teacher

◆ pens or pencils

◆ colored markers or crayons, optional

Activity—Part 1:

Tell the students . . . We rarely take the time to tell people why we like them. Some people probably think it is embarrassing—not quite cool. So, in order to make it easier, we are going to write down the reasons we like the people in this class.

(Model the activity as described below and then pass out page 17 sheets to the students.)

Explain to the students that when they receive their activity sheets, they will be writing their names on the line below the face, and then they will need to draw in their hair. Next, they will pass their papers to their neighbors. (Describe your passing pattern around the room.) When a student receives a paper, he or she needs to read the name and decide on a word that finishes the sentence at the top of the page: "I like you because you are_____ ." He or she will then write the word inside and around the outline of the face and pass the paper to the next person. Students will need to write small enough so that everyone will have room to add a word. Remind the students that only positive comments are allowed.

Activity—Part 2:

When the papers get back to their owners, give your students enough time to read and enjoy what was written about them. Let them share the comments if they want to. It would be nice to three-hole punch the papers and have the students keep them in the front of their notebooks so that they can be reminded on a daily basis of how the other people in the class feel about them.

Evaluation and Processing:

Discuss the activity . . . How did you feel when you read the comments? Did the words make you feel good about yourself and about how other people in the class think about you? Would you like to keep this paper where you can see it?

Growing in Social Awareness

Qualities: I Like You Because . . .

Directions: Check the name below the face. Then choose a word to complete this sentence and write the word inside or around the outline of the face.

"I like you because you are . . . _____ ."

Name

Growing in Social Awareness

Similarities and Differences: Everybody Counts

Purpose:

to introduce students to the people and cultures of four different countries through the numbers they use

Materials:

- ◆ *Count Your Way Through the Arab World* by Jim Haskins (Carolrhoda Books, 1991)
- ◆ *Count Your Way Through China* by Jim Haskins (Carolrhoda Books, 1987)
- ◆ *Count Your Way Through Japan* by Jim Haskins (Carolrhoda Books, 1987)
- ◆ *Count Your Way Through Mexico* by Jim Haskins (Carolrhoda Books, 1989)
- ◆ wall map of the world and/or globe
- ◆ copies of page 21 for reference page 21, one for each student
- ◆ copies of page 19, one for each student
- ◆ copies of page 20, one for each student
- ◆ pens or pencils

Activity—Part 1:

Spread this activity out over a week. Each book is 22 pages long, just right for one day. Use the map and/or globe to locate the geographical areas. Teach the numbers of each culture from one to ten. Discuss the cultures. Make the books available to students for spare-time reading.

Activity—Part 2:

Divide the class into four groups and give one of the books to each group. Pass out page 19 and 20. Ask your students to discuss and complete the activity sheets, passing the books around from group to group.

When the activity sheets have been completed, meet again as a large group. Have the students read the numbers aloud, using the pronunciations they wrote. Let the students share and discuss the facts they included in "Compare the Customs." Discuss the similarities and differences.

Evaluation and Processing:

Discuss the activity . . . Why does everybody count? Why is counting necessary?

Growing in Social Awareness

Similarities and Differences: Everybody Counts

Name_____ Date _____

Directions: Write the numerals, number words, and pronunciations for the numbers 1–10 for each culture.

Arab World	China
Japan	Mexico

Growing in Social Awareness

Similarities and Differences: Everybody Counts *(cont.)*

Name _____ Date _____

Directions: Write one fact about each topic for the four cultures named below.

Arab World	China
1. Mecca	1. dynasties
2. Kaaba	2. porcelain
3. Muhammad	3. The Great Wall
4. Allah	4. musical scale
Japan	**Mexico**
1. Mt. Fuji	1. Pyramid of the Sun
2. kimonos	2. Aztecs
3. chopsticks	3. Spanish conquistadors
4. sumo wrestling	4. The Volador

Growing in Social Awareness

Similarities and Differences: Everybody Counts

Use this chart for reference.

Numbers	Italian	Hindi	Spanish	Norwegian
1	uno	ek	uno	en
2	due	do	dos	tp
3	tre	teen	tres	tr
4	quattro	chaar	cuatro	fire
5	cinque	paanch	cinco	fem
6	sei	chhe	seis	seks
7	sette	saat	siete	sju
8	otto	aaTH	ocho	atte
9	nove	nau	nueve	ni
10	dieci	das	diez	ti
Numbers	**Japanese**	**German**	**French**	**Mandarin Chinese**
1	ee-CHEE	eins	un	yi
2	nee	zwei	deux	er
3	sahn	drei	trois	san
4	shee/yohn	vier	quatre	sz
5	goh	fünf	cinq	wu
6	roh-KOO	sechs	six	lyou
7	shee-CHEE	sieben	sept	chi
8	hah-CHEE	acht	huit	ba
9	joo	neun	neuf	jyou
10	joo	zehn	dix	shr

Growing in Social Awareness

Our Manners: In the Fifth Grade

Purpose:

to reinforce the idea that good manners make the classroom, as well as the world, a better place to be and to identify special reasons for having good manners in the fifth grade

Materials:

- ◆ copies of page 23, one for each student
- ◆ pens or pencils

Activity—Part 1:

Divide the students into groups to discuss the reasons for having good manners in a fifth grade classroom: What are good classroom manners? Why are they important? What are the benefits of good manners? Are there any special reasons for having good manners in the fifth grade?

Come together again in a large group and compare the results of the small group discussions.

Activity—Part 2:

Pass out the writing prompt (page 23). Give your students ample time to think and write. If you use the writing process, this can be a "quick write" or a first draft. Then give the students the opportunity to later do the editing and revising steps.

When the papers are completed (for your purposes), ask for volunteers to read their pieces aloud to the group. Remind the audience of good listening manners and the necessity for making positive comments.

Evaluation and Processing:

Discuss the activity . . . Were there any special reasons identified for having good manners in the fifth grade? Were the reasons for having good manners generally the same for all of the groups? Have you become more aware of your manners in dealing with one another?

Growing in Social Awareness

Our Manners: In the Fifth Grade

Name_____ Date _____

Writing Situation:

We have been discussing good manners at the fifth grade level. Your small group identified some reasons for having good classroom manners. You may have additional reasons of your own.

Directions for Writing:

Pick one (or more) of the reasons for having good manners and write about it (or them). Explain the effects that good manners have on you and the people around you. Express your thoughts in complete sentences. If you need more space, continue writing on the back of this paper.

_____

_____

_____

_____

_____

_____

_____

_____

_____

_____

_____

_____

_____

_____

Acquiring Communication Skills

Sending: I Feel . . .

Purpose:

to give students information about, and practice in, sending clear messages when they communicate orally, especially about a conflict situation

Materials:

◆ none necessary

Activity—Part 1:

This activity is designed to help your students accept the following ideas. Conflict is normal. They have the right to say how they feel and what they want. They will communicate more easily if they learn to express themselves in "*I*" messages rather than "*You*" messages. "*You*" messages use words that attack and blame. Here are some "*You*" messages:

◆ You always interrupt me and make me forget what I was going to say!

◆ You never ask before you borrow something from me!

"*I*" messages express the feelings of the person who is speaking. To facilitate the use of "*I*" messages, teach your students to use this formula:

I feel_____when _____
_____.
I want _____
_____.

Have your students practice turning "*You*" messages into "*I*" messages. Use the samples above and make up some of your own. Here are some possible "*I*" messages for the "*You*" messages given above:

◆ I feel frustrated when you interrupt me because it makes me forget what I wanted to say. I want to finish what I am saying without being interrupted.

◆ I feel angry when you borrow something of mine without asking. I want to be asked beforehand so that I can decide.

Acquiring Communication Skills

Sending: I Feel . . . *(cont.)*

Activity—Part 2:

When the opportunity arises in your classroom, have your students rephrase their actual *"You"* messages into *"I"* messages. It will take a lot of practice for your students to overcome what is probably a habit. Listen for students who are attacking one another with *"You"* messages like these:

"YOU" MESSAGES	"I" MESSAGE SUBSTITUTES
Why do you always bump into my desk when you go by? You always make me mess up my work.	I feel so angry when you bump my desk and my work gets messed up. I want you to be more careful.
You promised to remember my book. You never do anything you say you will do.	I feel disappointed because you forgot my book. I want you to do what you say you will do.

Evaluation and Processing:

Discuss the activity . . . Was it hard for you to learn to change *"You"* messages into *"I"* messages? Were you in the habit of expressing yourself with *"You"* messages? Have you tried to use *"I"* messages on your own? If not, do you plan to? If you have, what kind of reaction did you get? Was the other person more or less cooperative than usual? What was your own reaction? Have you gotten used to saying how you feel?

(Make sure that you model *"I"* messages constantly. It is not fair to say, "This class is always noisy! You embarrass me in front of the other teachers." Rephrase your message into an "I" message.)

I feel_____when _____
_____.
I want _____
_____.

Acquiring Communication Skills

Receiving: I Hear . . .

Purpose:

to give students information about, and practice in, active listening in order to enhance the communication process

Materials:

- ◆ copies of page 27, one for each student
- ◆ pens or pencils

Activity—Part 1:

The first step in active listening is repeating what was said. An easy way to teach active listening is simply to reverse the formula for an "*I*" message.

> You feel_____when _____
> _____.
> You want _____
> _____.

You can then add the second step which is rephrasing the information to show that it was understood.

"*I*" message: I hate it when you tease me about my freckles. I want you to stop.

Active listening: You hate it when I tease you about your freckles. You want me to stop.

Message restated: You want me to stop teasing you about your freckles because you hate it.

Activity—Part 2:

Have your students work in small groups to complete page 27. They can make up their own "*I*" messages, then write statements of active listening with the reverse formula, and finally restate what they heard in their own words. When everyone has completed the task, get together in a large group and read the "Reversing the Formula" pages out loud and discuss.

Evaluation and Processing:

Watch the students to see if they have internalized the active listening habit. You can see this in the ways people share in your class. ("I feel happy because my mother said I can have a birthday party." Is the general response "You are saying that you feel happy?" or "Who are you going to invite?")

Acquiring Communication Skills

Receiving: I Hear . . .

Name_____ Date _____

Directions: Make up a conflict situation and express it in the "I" message formula. Then, write what an active listener might hear by reversing the formula. Finally, restate the message. Use additional paper to make up other situations and repeat this process.

"I" Message

I feel_____when _____

_____.

I want_____

_____.

Active Listening—Reversed Formula

You feel_____when _____

_____.

You want _____

_____.

Restated Message

_____

_____

_____

_____

Acquiring Communication Skills

Responding: I Can . . .

Purpose:

to give students information about, and practice in, using a variety of listening responses

Materials:

- ◆ one enlarged or overhead transparency copy of page 30
- ◆ copies of page 31, one for each student
- ◆ pens or pencils

Activity—Part 1:

Give the students the following information . . . There is more than one kind of oral message and more than one style of listening. Sometimes people talk about facts and opinions rather than feelings, and sometimes we are not able to listen actively in the sense of repeating out loud what we hear. Nevertheless, the person sending the message must state it clearly, the person receiving the message must understand it, and there must be some response or feedback to make the communication process work.

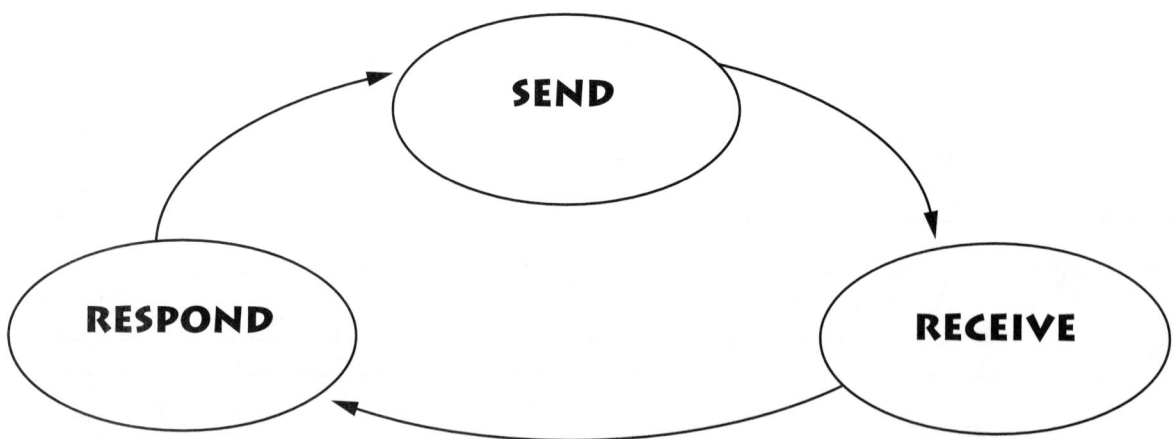

When the sender/speaker is talking about facts and opinions, they need to be organized and delivered in such a way that the receiver/listener can take them in. The receiver/listener (also called the audience) then has the responsibility of trying to understand what is being said. This comprehension must then be communicated back to the speaker. How can this be done?

After you have discussed the above information, ask your students to prepare short talks on any subjects that interest them. This will be most effective if they talk about something that is important to them, something they want the other people in the class to know about too. In giving their talks to the class, they will be "sending" facts and opinions rather than feelings.

Acquiring Communication Skills

Responding: I Can . . . *(cont.)*

Have the students discuss their responsibilities as speakers. They should try to make their talks clear and organized, speak in voices that can be heard, and try to establish eye contact with members of their audience.

Ask your students to discuss their responsibilities as listeners. They should be quiet and attentive, have a positive attitude toward the speaker and the information, and try to take in what is being said. They should be silent, "active listeners," repeating the information to themselves inside their heads.

Before beginning the presentation of the speeches, discuss the ways the audience might respond. The two main audience responses (excluding the clapping at the end of the speech) are eye contact and body language.

Eye contact:	This is as much a part of responding as it is of sending. The speaker who is trying to establish eye contact does not have a chance to do so if everyone in the audience is looking at the ceiling or out the window.
Body language:	This response is really important. It lets the speaker know that you are interested. Appropriate body language while listening and responding to a speaker can include both posture and gestures. For example, an audience member who leans forward slightly (posture) and nods his or her head (gesture) at important points is giving a positive response.

Ask the students to brainstorm some possible negative responses (leaning back, looking around or at the ceiling, yawning, staring blankly straight ahead, etc.).

Activity—Part 2:

Set aside an afternoon, or an hour on several afternoons, for the presentation of the speeches. After all of the speeches have been presented, have the students fill out the two checklists on page 31. The top one on page 31 is from the point of view of the speaker, and the bottom one is from the point of view of the audience. Compare and discuss the results.

Evaluation and Processing:

Discuss the activity . . . Which part of this activity did you like best—speaking, listening, learning about a new way to respond, or using the checklists? Which was the easiest? hardest? most fun? If you did this again, is there anything you would do differently?

Acquiring Communication Skills

Responding: I Can . . .

Teacher Directions: Enlarge this chart (or make an overhead transparency copy) and use it during discussions about communication.

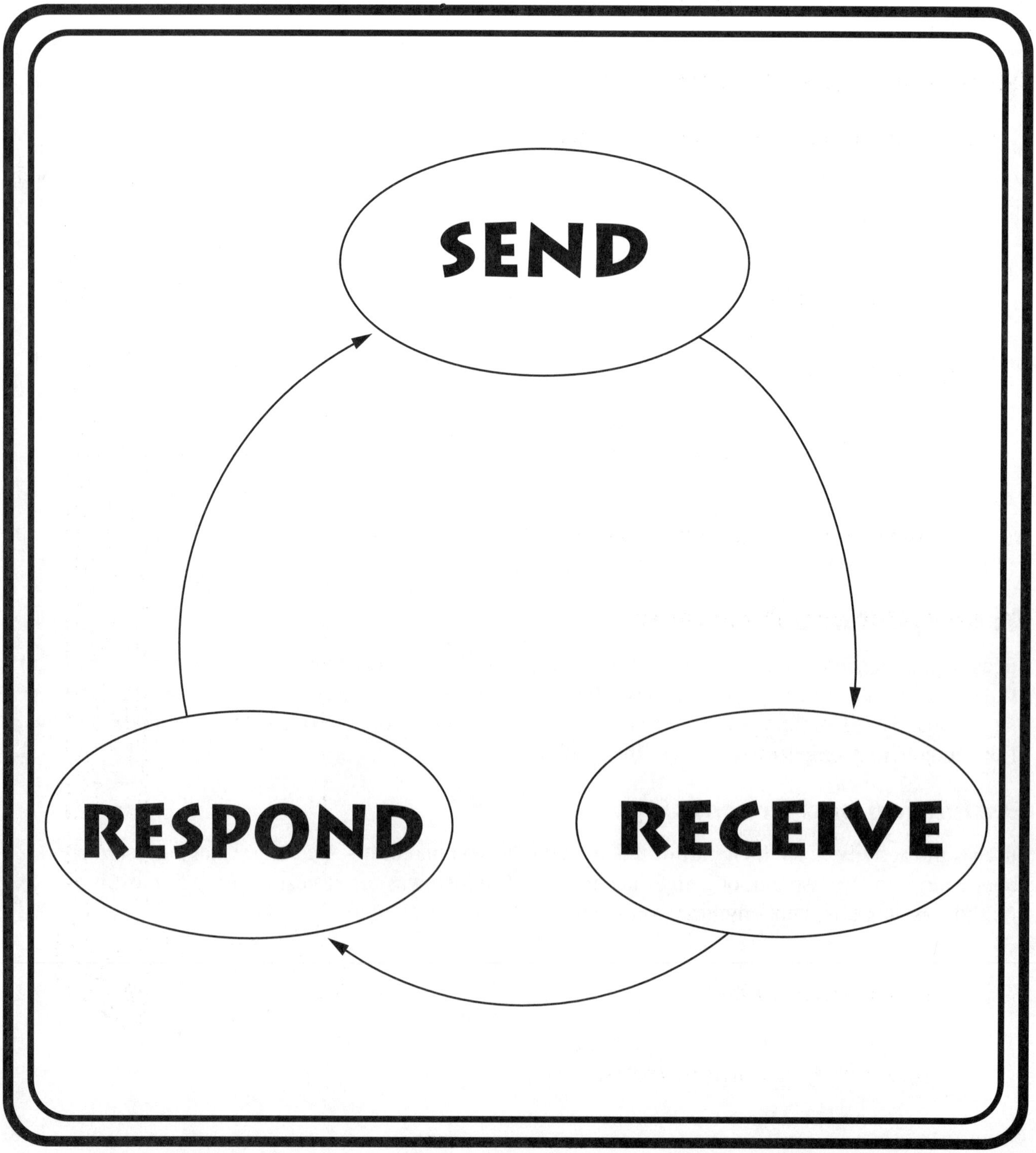

SEND

RECEIVE

RESPOND

Acquiring Communication Skills

Responding: I Can . . .

Name_____ Date _____

Directions: Analyze your participation in this speech activity. Check off the boxes which pertain to your experience.

When I Was the Speaker

I felt as if the audience heard me because . . .

☐ . . . no one talked.

☐ . . . they looked interested.

☐ . . . they looked at me.

☐ . . . I was able to make eye contact.

☐ . . . they nodded at the important points.

When I Was the Audience:

I responded by . . .

☐ . . . paying attention.

☐ . . . looking interested.

☐ . . . looking at the speaker.

☐ . . . making eye contact.

☐ . . . nodding at important points.

Developing Respect and Empathy

I Know What You Mean: Immigration

Purpose:

to give students information about the problems faced by immigrants both as immigrants and emigrants

Materials:

◆ *Molly's Pilgrim* by Barbara Cohen (Lothrop, Lee & Shepard Books, 1983), five or six copies, if possible

◆ copies of page 33, one for each student

◆ pens or pencils

Activity—Part 1:

Read *Molly's Pilgrim* aloud to the class. It is a very short book and can easily be read in one sitting. Discuss the story. Ask students to respond to the following questions: Why did Molly's family come to the United States? (They came to escape religious persecution.) Why did they leave New York City? (They left the city to escape poor working and living conditions.) Why did Molly stop telling her mama about what went on in school? (Molly stopped to keep her from talking to the teacher.)

Activity—Part 2:

Pass out the copies of page 33 Divide the students into small groups to work on this activity sheet. Give each group a copy of the book to use as a reference. (If you have enough copies of the book, all the groups can do this activity at the same time. If you do not have extra copies, have one group complete this activity at a time while the other students complete another activity.)

Evaluation and Processing:

Discuss the activity . . . Why did some of the students make fun of Molly? Why do some people think that it is bad to be different? Has anyone ever made fun of you or of someone you know because of religious beliefs or the way he or she looked or talked?

If someone did make fun of you for any of those reasons, could you send an *"I"* message to him or her about it? (Ask for volunteers to describe situations and make up appropriate *"I"* messages.)

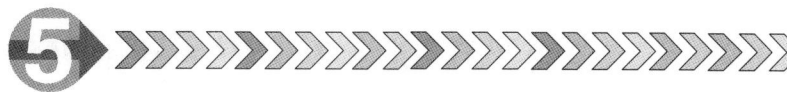

Developing Respect and Empathy

I Know What You Mean: Immigration

Name_____ Date _____

Directions: Read the quotations from *Molly's Pilgrim* in the left column. Then, in the right column, describe the meanings of each of the quotations.

What Was Said	What Was Meant
Molly said, "They all admired Elizabeth. She brought peppermint sticks to school and handed them out to all her friends at recess."	
Molly said, "Mama, let's go back to New York City."	
Molly said, "I didn't want Miss Stickley or Elizabeth to see Mama."	
Elizabeth said, "I guess you people don't celebrate American holidays."	
Mama said, "That's me, Molly. I'm a Pilgrim!"	
Miss Stickley said, "The Pilgrims got the idea for Thanksgiving from Jews like Molly and her mama."	
Molly said, "I decided . . . it was all right for Mama to come to school.	

Developing Respect and Empathy

I Know How You Feel: Immigration

Purpose:

to give students information about the problems faced by immigrants both as immigrants and emigrants

Materials:

◆ *Molly's Pilgrim* by Barbara Cohen (Lothrop, Lee & Shepard Books, 1983), five or six copies, if possible

◆ masking tape

◆ sweaters, coats, scarves, etc.

◆ copies of page 37, one for each student

◆ pens or pencils

Activity—Part 1:

Tell the students . . . The family in *Molly's Pilgrim* probably came to this country by boat through some very difficult conditions that are hard for us to imagine from just reading about them. (Do the "Immigration Simulation" on page 35.)

Activity—Part 2:

Tell the students . . . When immigrants finally arrived in the United States, many would land at Ellis Island. (Read the information and do the Ellis Island simulation on page 36.)

Activity—Part 3:

Pass out the activity sheet (page 37). Have the students complete it individually. When all of the students have finished, meet in a large group to compare and discuss the choices they made.

Evaluation and Processing:

Discuss the activity . . . Did the simulations give you a better idea of the hardships immigrants suffered? Many people over the years have gone through difficult experiences of one kind or another to get to this country. Why? Does anyone in your family have a story to tell about immigrating to this country? If so, would they be willing to share it with our class?

Developing Respect and Empathy

I Know How You Feel: Immigration

Set the Stage:

The family in *Molly's Pilgrim's* probably came to the United States by boat. Since they came from Russia, they probably came in a large ship, perhaps in steerage class. (Have someone look up *steerage* and read the definition to the class.) The immigrants would have been crowded into dark, smelly areas. They would have slept on narrow bunk beds. Their trip would have taken place sometime in the late 1800s to the early 1900s when Jews were the targets of religious persecution in Russia. (Have someone look up *persecution* and read the definition to the class.)

Begin the Simulation:

◆ Use masking tape to mark off a small area on the floor (about 4' x 6' or 1.2 m x 1.8 m).

◆ Ask the students to put on several layers of clothing such as sweaters and coats.

◆ Have them each carry several small objects such as books, toys, or lunch boxes.

◆ Begin by putting a comfortable number of students into the area. Let them sit down. Tell them they may not move out of the marked area.

◆ Gradually begin to add more students to the area. Tell them to also sit down.

◆ Remind everyone that he or she must not move out of the marked area.

◆ Ask a few students to try to take off a coat or a sweater. Have others try to turn around.

◆ End the simulation when the students seem restless and uncomfortable, but make sure everyone has had a turn. Repeat the same simulation with the students who did not have a chance the first time.

Discuss the Experience:

◆ How would people feel if they had to stay that crowded for very long?

◆ How did you feel during the short time you were so crowded?

◆ What would have happened if someone had become seasick?

◆ Why did people put up with those conditions?

Developing Respect and Empathy

I Know How You Feel: Immigration

Ellis Island was an immigrant processing center that was open from 1892 until 1952. During that time, over 12 million immigrants entered the United States through Ellis Island. Today, more than four out of every ten American people can trace their roots to an ancestor who entered America through Ellis Island. Built to process 5,000 new immigrants each day, it often processed twice that number.

Once the immigrants stepped off their boats, large numbered tags were tied to their clothing. They were taken to the registry hall where, after waiting in long lines, they were examined by doctors. Chalk marks were put on their clothing if any medical problems were suspected. Anyone whose clothing was marked was detained for further examination. About one out of every six people was delayed for as long as four days because of medical problems, and one out of every ten of those delayed was sent back to his or her homeland because the problem was judged to be serious. Those who made it past the medical examination were then questioned by a government inspector. If any answer was suspect, the person would face a board of special inquiry who would decide if the person could stay. If all tests were passed, the immigrants average stay on Ellis Island was about five hours.

Simulation:

Have the students reenact a group of immigrants' arrival to Ellis Island. All of the students will be immigrants except for nine students who will play the roles described below.

Have one student hand out tags with numbers to be taped to the immigrants' clothing. One student will act as the medical examiner. He or she will carefully look in the immigrants' eyes, ears, and mouths. The medical examiner may choose about one out of every five immigrants to see the specialist. The person acting as the medical specialist will determine whether the immigrant should be sent back or allowed to remain. The immigrants who pass the medical examination will then be sent to the government inspector. This person will choose to ask each immigrant some of the following questions:

What is your name?
How old are you? Are you married?
What is your occupation? Can you read or write?
Where are you from?
Where are you going to in the United States? How will you get there?
Did you pay for your passage? If not, who did?
How much money do you have with you?
Do you have any relatives in the United States? What are the names and addresses of your relatives?
Have you ever been to the United States before? When and where?
Have you ever been in prison?
How is your health?

Any immigrant who seems unsure of an answer will be sent to a special inquiry board made up of five students who will continue to ask similar questions. At the end of the questioning, they will vote to determine whether the person will be allowed to remain in the United States. Follow the simulation with a discussion.

Developing Respect and Empathy

I Know How You Feel: Immigration

In *Molly's Pilgrim*, Molly's family immigrates to America. In leaving their native land, they leave behind many of the things that are important to them. In a very short time they must make decisions about what few, small items they wish to take with them. It is your turn now to make some decisions. Besides the necessities what would you take with you if you suddenly had to leave this country? Would it be something you would play with on the trip? Maybe it would be your favorite book. Perhaps you would choose a gift someone special gave to you. Choose carefully. You may take only five items, and they must fit into a backpack. You will be responsible for carrying them.

Directions: Write your choices and your reasons for them in the chart below.

Choice	Reason

Sixth Grade

Developing Self-Concepts

My Name: Why So Many Names?

Purpose:

to give students some information about names, the different kinds there are and why they are so important to people

Materials:

- encyclopedias and other reference materials
- copies of page 40, one for each student
- copies of page 41, one for each student
- pencils or pens

Activity—Part 1:

Let the students work as partners or in small groups to research information for the activity on page 40. Read it through with them before they begin and pronounce the word *pseudonym* for them. Have everybody say it a few times. When they have completed their activity sheets, meet back in a large group and compare their results. Discuss.

Ask your students . . . What is your surname? What is your given name? Do you have a middle name? Do you have a nickname? Do you use your nickname just at home or all the time? If you took a pseudonym, what would it be? Why?

Activity—Part 2:

Pass out copies of page 41. Give your students ample time to think and write. If you use the writing process, this can be a "quick write" or a first draft. Then give the students the opportunity to later do the editing and revising steps.

When the papers are completed (for your purposes), ask for volunteers to read their pieces aloud to the group. Remind the audience of good listening manners and the necessity for making positive comments.

Evaluation and Processing:

Discuss Part 1 of the activity . . . What did you learn that you did not already know? Did you learn anything that might apply to your own name? Was your group easy to work with? How did you share the tasks?

Discuss Part 2 of the activity . . . Was it fun to choose a pseudonym? Had you ever thought about doing that before? Many movie stars use pseudonyms. Do you know of any currently popular stars who are using pseudonyms? Do you know of any writers who are best known by their pen names?

Answers for Page 40	
1. given, Christian	5. Revolutionary War
2. family, surnames	6. nicknames
3. Chinese	7. pen name, nom de plume, stage name, alias
4. places, jobs, ancestors (for example, Hill, Baker, Jackson)	

Developing Self-Concepts

My Name: Why So Many Names?

Student _____ Date _____

Partner Name or Group Members:_____

Directions: Use an encyclopedia, dictionary, or other resource and the words in the Word Bank to fill in the blanks below.

1. First names are sometimes called_____names or_____names.

2. Last names can be called_____names or_____.

3. The_____were the first people to use more than one name.

4. Many last names developed from names of_____,

   _____, and_____.

5. Middle names were not common in the United States until after the

   _____.

6. Short names or pet names are called_____.

7. Pseudonyms are names used to protect a person's real identity. A writer's pseudonym is a

   _____or_____. An actor's pseudonym is a_____.

   A criminal's pseudonym is an_____.

Word Bank

stage name	Chinese	Revolutionary War	ancestors
places	given	alias	nom de plume
nicknames	pen name	Christian	
family	jobs	surnames	

Developing Self-Concepts

My Name: Why So Many Names?

Name_____ Date _____

Writing Situation

Pretend you are an actor or writer. You think you are going to become very famous and you want to choose a pseudonym to protect your privacy. It has to be one you really like because it might stick with you for a long time.

Directions for Writing:

Write about the stage name or pen name you would choose for yourself. Tell your reasons for choosing it and why you think it is a good name. Express your thoughts in complete sentences. If you need more space, continue writing on the back of this paper.

_____

_____

_____

_____

_____

_____

_____

_____

_____

_____

_____

_____

Developing Self-Concepts

How I Look: If I Had a Hundred Dollars to Spend on Clothes

Purpose:

to give students the opportunity to explore the relationship between the clothes they would like to own and how they feel about themselves

Materials:

- copies of newspaper sections that contain advertisements for clothes, one set for each student, if possible (Your local newspaper may be willing to give you a classroom set.)
- large pieces of construction paper
- drawing paper

- scissors
- glue sticks
- markers
- pens or pencils
- copies of page 43, one for each student

Activity—Part 1:

Tell and ask the students . . . Many students your age like to go to malls and shop for clothing. Are you one of these people? Do you have a favorite store? Do you like to try things on? Do you shop by yourself, with a parent, or with a friend? If you do not shop by yourself, would you like to?

If you had enough money, is there some piece of clothing you would like to buy? Have you looked at it in the stores or in advertisements?

Share, compare, and discuss the ideas.

Activity—Part 2:

Tell the students . . . Pretend you have a hundred dollars to spend on clothes. Place your sheet of construction paper horizontally and fold it in half like a book. Then look through the newspaper advertisements and see if you can find a picture or pictures of what you would like to buy. Cut out the pictures and the prices of the items and glue them onto the left side of your sheet of construction paper. If you cannot find a picture of what you want, draw it on another piece of paper and then cut out your drawing or drawings and glue them onto the construction paper. Write your best estimate of the prices.

Complete the activity on page 43 and glue it to the right side of the construction paper.

Evaluation and Processing:

Discuss the activity . . . How much do you want the item(s) you found and wrote about? a little? a lot? Would you be willing to give up something else? What?

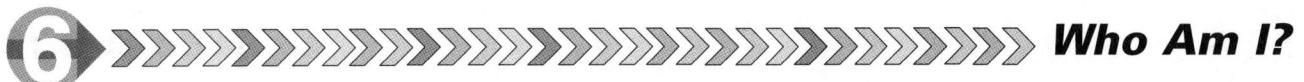

Developing Self-Concepts

How I Look: If I Had a Hundred Dollars to Spend on Clothes

Name_____ Date _____

Directions: Pretend someone just gave you a hundred dollars to spend on clothing. Take a minute to think about what you would buy. Share your thoughts on the lines below.

I want to buy_____

because _____

_____

_____

_____.

If I had it, I would feel_____

_____

_____

_____

_____.

Clothes are important because _____

_____

_____

_____

_____.

Developing Self-Concepts

What I Know: Twenty Things That I Know

Purpose:

to give students the opportunity to think about and express some of the things they know that are not related to school

Materials:

- ◆ copies of page 45, one for each student
- ◆ pens or pencils

Activity—Part 1:

Begin this activity as one large group. Ask your students to think about the things that they do outside of school—things they do with their parents, brothers and sisters, other relatives, friends, neighbors, coaches, and by themselves. Ask them to think about the hobbies they have, the lessons they take, and the places they go. Are they really good at something that is never mentioned in school?

Pass out page 45 and give your students ample time to think while they fill it out. Encourage them to think of enough things to fill in all twenty blanks. Collect the lists and put them aside for Part 2 of this activity.

Activity—Part 2:

Have the students take turns reading their lists out loud to the class. If students seem particularly interested in an item, make a note. When the sharing has been completed, discuss with the students the different accomplishments they have heard about.

Ask if any of the students would be willing to teach a skill to the others. If this is a popular idea, help your students to set up some miniclasses for interested groups. Make available sign-up sheets and set aside a period for groups to meet with their instructors. Students who are not interested in joining a group can read or pursue some other individual activity.

Evaluation and Processing:

Discuss Part 1 of the activity . . . Were you surprised that you know so many things? Was it hard or easy to list twenty things? Were you surprised at the things other students listed?

Discuss Part 2 of the activity . . . If you taught a skill to a group, how did that feel? Was it hard? easy? fun? Would you like to do it again? If you attended a group, how did that feel? Did you enjoy it? Would you like to do it again? If you both taught and attended a group, which did you enjoy more?

Developing Self-Concepts

What I Know: Twenty Things That I Know

Name _____ Date _____

Directions: Think of twenty things that you know that your classmates may not know about you. Consider your hobbies and activities outside of school and interesting facts about yourself. Try to compile a list which represents more than one aspect of your life (for example, do not only list sports that you are involved in).

1. _____
2. _____
3. _____
4. _____
5. _____
6. _____
7. _____
8. _____
9. _____
10. _____
11. _____
12. _____
13. _____
14. _____
15. _____
16. _____
17. _____
18. _____
19. _____
20. _____

Developing Self-Concepts

How I Feel: I Am Confused About What Is Happening

Purpose:

to give students information and answer questions about the physical changes (e.g., rapid growth spurts) that they are experiencing

Materials:

◆ copies of page 47, one for each student

◆ pens or pencils

Note: Physical changes during the sixth grade are certainly connected to puberty, and you may want to deal with these issues as part of your regular sex education program, the parameters of which are probably mandated by your school district. However, students are often worried about the peripheral issues such as skin problems, voice changes, and rapid growth spurts—concerns that might be dealt with here as part of their developing self-concepts. In this activity, students will examine how they feel about sudden growth spurts.

Activity—Part 1:

Say to the students . . . During the sixth grade, some people start to grow very fast, and some people do not. That is very normal and perfectly okay in the long run, but it can be very confusing. One day you and your best friend are more or less the same size, and almost overnight, it seems, one of you is a head taller than the other. This can have an effect on your social life, your participation in sports teams, and your self-esteem.

Activity—Part 2:

Pass out copies page 47. Give your students ample time to think and write. If you use the writing process, this can be a "quick write" or a first draft. Then give the students the opportunity to later do the editing and revising steps.

When the papers are completed (for your purposes), ask for volunteers to read their pieces aloud to the group. Remind the audience of good listening manners and the necessity for making positive comments.

Although this writing situation was designed to be a fictional one, some of the students in your class may have actually had this experience. Ask if anyone wants to comment on a real experience that resembled the one in the writing situation. Discuss.

Evaluation and Processing:

Discuss the activity . . . What can you do when something over which you have no control affects your self-esteem? In this case, would it help the two friends to realize that the situation was only temporary? Why or why not?

Developing Self-Concepts

How I Feel: I Am Confused About What Is Happening

Name_____ Date _____

Writing Situation:

You and your best friend have always been about the same size. You were away all summer and did not see your friend again until the first day of school in the fall. You were not the same size anymore. In fact, there was a difference of about a foot in your heights.

Directions for Writing:

Write about how this would make you feel. Would you be the tall one or the short one? Could your friendship survive the effect of this sudden and unexpected difference? Express your thoughts clearly and in complete sentences. If you need more space, continue writing on the back of this paper.

_____

_____

_____

_____

_____

_____

_____

_____

_____

_____

_____

_____

Growing in Social Awareness

Names: I Miss You

Purpose:

to give every student the opportunity to learn the names of all of the other students in the class and to associate the names with the right people

Materials:

- ◆ multiple copies of the class roster to be used as roll sheets
- ◆ multiple copies of the seating chart to be used as roll sheets
- ◆ copies of page 49, one for each student
- ◆ pens or pencils

Activity—Part 1:

This part of the activity can simply be part of your classroom management plan. Just set up a daily routine during which one student takes the roll. Start by having student roll-takers call the names of the students out loud. As each person's name is called, that person should raise his or her hand and say "Here." The roll-taker should look up each time in order to associate the name with the person who answers. Rotate this roll-taking assignment until everyone in the class has had at least one turn.

After everyone has had a turn to call the roll, have the roll-taker do the job silently, using a seating chart rather than a class list or together with a class list. This may be difficult at first, and the person taking the roll may need to double-check by calling out some names. Rotate this assignment also until everyone in the class has had at least one turn.

Activity—Part 2:

Tell the students . . . It is impossible to miss people if you do not know they are a part of the class to begin with. However, you may find that you miss people who are absent now that you know who they are.

Pass out the writing prompt (page 49). Give your students ample time to think and write. If you use the writing process, this can be a "quick write" or a first draft. Then give the students the opportunity to later do the editing and revising steps.

When the papers are completed (for your purposes), ask for volunteers to read their pieces aloud to the group. Remind the audience of good listening manners and the necessity for making positive comments.

Evaluation and Processing:

Test your students on the names they know. Have a contest to see who can call the most people by their correct names. Discuss the advantages of knowing the names of everyone in the class. What are the benefits? Do you enjoy having other people call you by your name? Would you say that you have more friends now than you did before?

Growing in Social Awareness

Names: I Miss You

Name_____ Date _____

Writing Situation:

We have been doing activities to help us become aware of which students are here and which ones are absent. Now that you know the people in this class by name, you may find that you miss the ones who are absent.

Directions for Writing:

Pick one of the people whose names you have recently learned and whom you would now miss if he or she were absent. Why would you miss this person? Would you have missed this person before? Express your thoughts in complete sentences. If you need more space, continue writing on the other side of this paper.

_____

_____

_____

_____

_____

_____

_____

_____

_____

_____

_____

_____

Growing in Social Awareness

Qualities: Our Class

Purpose:

to encourage students to become aware of and appreciate the good qualities of their classmates as a group

Materials:

- ◆ an enlarged copy of page 51, glued onto a piece of poster board for classroom display
- ◆ wide-tipped felt pens in a variety of colors
- ◆ scratch paper
- ◆ thesaurus and/or dictionary
- ◆ laminating materials (clear shelf paper will work)

Activity—Part 1:

Tell the students . . . Think of the people in our class as a group. What words come to your minds to describe us? Are we friendly? helpful? studious? funny? What words can you think of?

Have your students discuss this as partners and come up with two words per partner/pair. Meet again as a large group and compare the results. Try to think of more words to replace any duplications (a thesaurus and dictionary may be useful for this).

Have the students practice writing their words on scratch paper. Suggest different kinds of letters to use: block capitals, balloon letters, italics, etc. Check that they correctly spell the words.

Have each student write the word he or she has chosen and practiced on the poster (inside the outline of the door).

Laminate and display the poster.

Activity—Part 2:

Have the students share the reasons behind their choices (e.g., "I chose the word *friendly* because when I came to this school, people in this class made me feel welcome.") These reasons can be written on strips of paper and displayed around the poster.

Evaluation and Processing:

Have students look at and read the completed poster. Ask them questions like these . . . Are you proud to be a member of a class that has these qualities? Does belonging to a class like this make school a more pleasant place to be?

Growing in Social Awareness

Qualities: Our Class

Teacher Directions: Enlarge this page and glue the copy onto a piece of poster board for classroom display. After the students have added words (see page 50), laminate the finished product.

The People in Our Class Are . . .

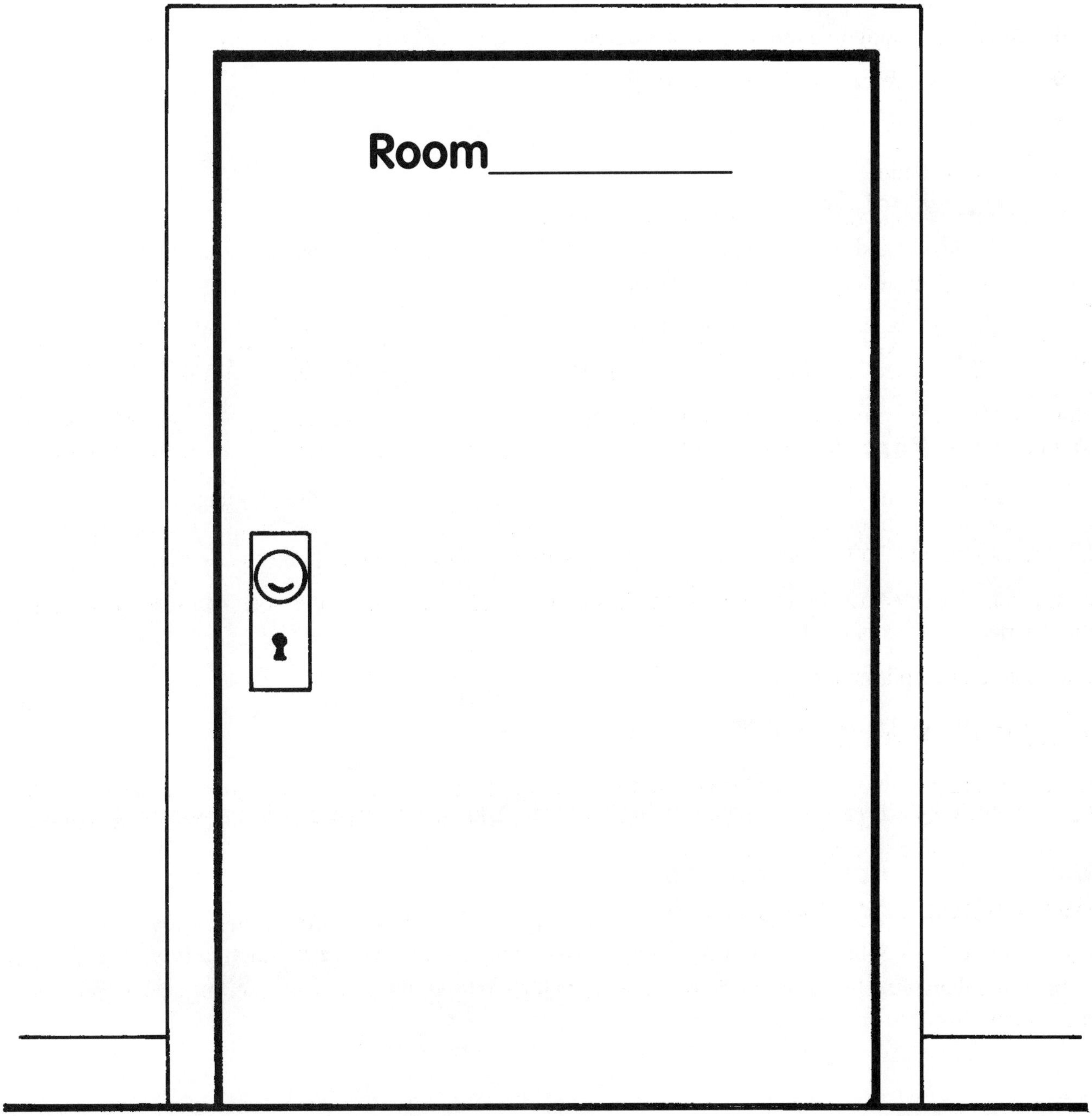

Room_____

Growing in Social Awareness

Similarities and Differences: Everybody Says Hello

Purpose:

to introduce students to different forms of greetings used around the world, the countries in which they are used, and the cultures they represent

Materials:

◆ copies of the page 53, one for each student

◆ a wall map of the world and/or a globe

◆ encyclopedias and other reference books

Activity—Part 1:

Greet your class in a different language every day. Distribute copies of page 53 so that students can use the greetings also. Practice the pronunciations together.

Look up the language of the day in an encyclopedia or another reference book. Find the location or locations in which the language is spoken on the map and/or globe. Learn some facts about the language.

Activity—Part 2:

Expand the lesson by doing an art activity associated with a place where the language is spoken.

Here are some examples:

Hawaii—crepe or tissue paper leis

Japan—folded paper fans

Africa—tribal masks

Mexico—papier-mâché piñatas

Near East—geometric designs

Display the art on a multicultural bulletin board. Add written greetings in the various languages.

Evaluation and Processing:

Discuss the activity . . . How many ways can you say "hello"? Have you tried these greetings outside of our classroom? What reaction did you get? Now that you can say "hello" in a variety of languages, is there any language you would like to learn to speak? Which one(s)?

Growing in Social Awareness

Similarities and Differences: Everybody Says Hello

Language	Greeting	Pronunciation
English	Hello	hel-LO
Spanish	Hola	OH-la
Hawaiian	Aloha	ah-LO-ha
Swahili	Jambo	JAHM-bo
French	Bonjour	bon-zhoor
Arabic	Salaam	sah-LAHM
Japanese	Konnichiwa	kon-nichi-WAH
Hindi	Namaste	nam-ahs-TAY
German	Guten Tag	GU-ten TAHG
Yiddish	Shalom	sha-LOHM
Russian	Priviet	preev-YET

Growing in Social Awareness

Our Manners: In Our School

Purpose:

to reinforce the idea that good manners make the school, as well as the world, a better place to be; to identify special reasons for having good manners in school as sixth graders

Materials:

- ◆ copies of page 55, one for each student
- ◆ pens or pencils

Activity—Part 1:

Divide your students into groups. Ask the groups to discuss why sixth graders should have good manners in school. What are good school manners? Why are they important? What are the benefits of good manners? Are there any special reasons for sixth graders to have good manners in school?

Then meet as a large group and compare the results of the small group discussions.

Activity—Part 2:

Pass out the writing prompt (page 55). Give your students ample time to think and write. If you use the writing process, this can be a "quick write" or a first draft. Then give the students the opportunity to later do the editing and revising steps.

When the papers are completed (for your purposes), ask for volunteers to read their pieces aloud to the group. Remind the audience of good listening manners and the necessity for making positive comments.

Evaluation and Processing:

Discuss the activity . . . Were there any special reasons identified for sixth graders to have good manners in school or were the reasons for having good manners generally the same for any grade level? Have your students become more aware of their manners in dealing with one another?

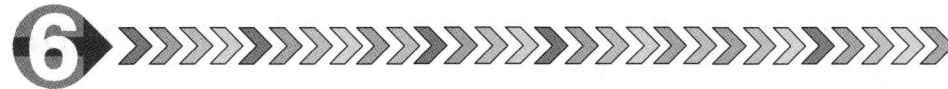

Growing in Social Awareness

Our Manners: In Our School

Name_____ Date _____

Writing Situation:

We have been discussing reasons for sixth graders to have good manners in school. Your small group identified some reasons and you may have some additional reasons, of your own.

Directions for Writing:

Pick one (or more) of the reasons for having good manners in school as a sixth grader and write about it (or them). Explain the effects that good manners have on you and the people around you. Express your thoughts in complete sentences. If you need more space, continue writing on the other side of this paper.

_____

_____

_____

_____

_____

_____

_____

_____

_____

_____

_____

_____

_____

Acquiring Communication Skills

Sending: I Feel . . .

Purpose:

to give students information about and practice in sending clear messages when they communicate orally, especially about a conflict situation

Materials:

◆ copies of pages 58 and 59, one set for each student

◆ pens or pencils

Activity—Part 1:

Depending on the experience that your students have had in sending "I" messages, you may want to use the lesson starting on page 24 in the fifth grade section before using the material presented here. As in fifth grade, this activity is designed to help the students accept the idea that conflict is normal and that they have the right to say how they feel and what they want. At the very least, they should be able to express themselves in "I" messages rather than "You" messages.

"You" messages are words that attack and blame:

◆ You never listen to the teacher! You expect me to explain everything to you!

◆ You are always in such a hurry to get out to recess that you nearly knock me down!

"I" messages express the feelings of the person who is speaking. To facilitate the use of "I" messages, teach your students to use the following formula:

I feel_____when _____

_____.

I want _____

_____.

Have the students practice turning "You" messages into "I" messages. Here are some sample "I" messages for the "You" messages given above.

◆ I feel used when you expect me to explain everything to you. I want you to listen to the teacher yourself.

◆ I feel angry when you nearly knock me down on your way to recess. I want you to slow down and be more careful.

Acquiring Communication Skills

Sending: I Feel . . . *(cont.)*

As in the fifth grade lesson, take every opportunity in your classroom to have your students rephrase their actual *"You"* messages into *"I"* messages. It will take a lot of practice for them to overcome what is probably a well-rehearsed habit. Listen for students who are attacking one another with *"You"* messages like these:

Why do you always try to copy my answers? You never do your own work!

(I feel angry when you copy my answers. I want you to do your own work.)

You promised to return the money I loaned to you. You do not keep your word.

(I feel very upset because you did not bring the money that you owe me. I want you to keep your word.)

Activity—Part 2:

When everyone has had ample oral practice, pass out the activity sheet entitled "You and I" and have the students complete it. This can be done individually, in partners, or in small groups. When everyone has completed the task, meet again as a large group to share and compare the answers and discuss ideas.

Evaluation and Processing:

Discuss the activity . . . Was it hard for you to learn to change *"You"* messages into *"I"* messages? Were you in the habit of expressing yourself with *"You"* messages? Have you tried to use *"I"* messages on your own? If not, do you plan to? If you have, what kind of reaction did you get? Was the other person more or less cooperative than usual? What was your own reaction? Have you gotten used to saying how you feel?

(Note: As was mentioned in the fifth grade lesson, be sure that you model *"I"* messages constantly. It is not fair to say, "You are all so messy! You make me feel embarrassed when I see the custodian." Rephrase your statement to make an *"I"* message.)

I feel_____when _____

_____.

I want _____

_____.

Acquiring Communication Skills

Sending: I Feel . . .

Name_____ Date _____

Directions: Write an *"I"* message for each *"You"* message.

1. You never stop talking! You keep me from hearing what the
   teacher is saying.

I feel_____when_____.

I want_____

_____.

2. You ask me for paper every day. You never have your own supplies.

I feel_____when _____.

I want _____

_____.

3. You always pick your best friends for your team. You never give
   anyone else a chance.

I feel_____when_____.

I want_____

_____.

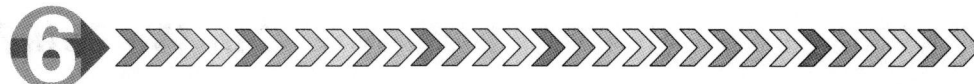

Acquiring Communication Skills

Sending: I Feel . . .

Name_____ Date _____

Directions: Write an *"I"* message for each *"You"* message.

4. You always say bad things about people. You tell me stuff that
   makes me feel uncomfortable.

I feel_____when_____.

I want_____

_____.

5. You don't do your share of the group work. You expect other
   people to do all of the work.

I feel_____when _____.

I want _____

_____.

6. You never clean your desk. Your stuff is all over the floor.

I feel_____when_____.

I want_____

_____.

Acquiring Communication Skills

Receiving: I Hear . . .

Purpose:

to give students information about and practice in active listening in order to enhance the communication process

Materials:

◆ copies of page 61, one for each student

◆ pens or pencils

Activity—Part 1:

If your students have not had practice in active listening, you may want to use the fifth grade lesson which starts on page 26 before proceeding. It is very structured and contains a formula to make it easy to repeat what was heard. (It can also be used for review, even if your students are familiar with active listening.) However, if your students are ready for a more sophisticated approach, proceed to Part 2 of this activity.

Activity—Part 2:

Tell the students . . . In real life, active listeners usually move past just repeating what they hear to restating it in their own words. This seems more natural, and it also shows whether or not the listener really understands what was said.

Here is a rather emotional *"I"* message:

> I feel like screaming when you poke me and pull my hair. I want you to keep your hands to yourself!

Here is the active listening "formula" response:

> You feel like screaming when I poke you and pull your hair. You want me to keep my hands to myself.

Here is a restatement showing that the listener really understands the message:

> You want me to stop poking you and pulling your hair because it makes you really, really angry.

Have your students work in small groups on "Restating the Information." They can make up their own *"I"* messages and then restate the messages to show understanding, leaving out the active listening "formula" response. When everyone has completed the task, get together in a large group to read and discuss their work.

Evaluation and Processing:

Watch your students to see if they have internalized the active listening habit. You can hear this when people exchange information. (For example, "I'm excited about going camping!" Is the general response, "You really seem happy about going camping!" or "Do you get to invite a friend?")

Acquiring Communication Skills

Receiving: I Hear . . .

Name_____ Date _____

Directions: Make up an *"I"* message and write it in the first section. Then, in the second section, restate the message as an active listener would.

"I" Message:

I feel_____when _____

_____.

I want _____

_____.

Message Restated:

_____

_____

_____

_____

If you have trouble with the restatement, use this formula and then try the restatement again.

Active Listening Formula:

You feel_____when _____.

You want _____

_____.

Use additional paper to create more *"I"* messages and restatements.

Acquiring Communication Skills

Responding: I Can . . .

Purpose:

to give students information about and practice in using a variety of listening responses

Materials:

◆ copies of the fifth grade lesson on pages 28–31, one set for each student

◆ copies of page 63, one for each student

◆ pens or pencils

Activity—Part 1:

Teach the entire "Responding: I Can . . ." lesson from the fifth grade section (pages 28–31).

Activity—Part 2:

Ask your students to consider how the new communication skills they have been learning and discussing could relate to the *"I"* messages and active listening skills that they have been practicing. Pass out the writing prompt (page 63), and give your students ample time to think and write. When they are through, ask for volunteers to share and compare their conclusions.

Evaluation and Processing:

Discuss the activity . . . What responsibilities do people have as speakers/senders? (They should try to make their ideas clear and organized, speak in voices that can be heard, and try to establish eye contact with members of their audience whether it consists of a group of people or just one person.) What responsibilities do people have as listeners/receivers? (They should be quiet and attentive, have a positive attitude toward the speaker and the information, and try to take in what is being said. They can also be silent, active listeners, repeating the information to themselves inside their heads.)

Responsibilities

Be quiet and attentive.

Take in what is being said.

Have a positive attitude toward the speaker.

6

Acquiring Communication Skills

Responding: I Can . . .

Name_____ Date _____

Writing Situation:

You have just finished learning and practicing some new communication skills: talking about facts and opinions, listening quietly and attentively, and responding with eye contact and body language.

Directions for Writing:

Write about ways in which these skills apply to what you already know about *"I"* messages and active listening. Do all of them apply? How can they be used? Be ready to share your ideas with the rest of the class.

_____

_____

_____

_____

_____

_____

_____

_____

_____

_____

_____

_____

Developing Respect and Empathy

I Know What You Mean: Different Is Okay

Purpose:
to give students the opportunity to think about differences as interesting rather than threatening

Materials:
◆ *The Hundred Dresses* by Eleanor Estes (Harcourt Brace Jovanovich, 1974)
◆ copies of page 65, one for each student
◆ copies of page 66, one for each student (Note: Copy this page onto stiff paper or glue it onto pieces of poster board so that it will be able to stand.)
◆ art materials, including different kinds of paper (tissue, crepe, construction), scraps of material and trimmings, yarn for hair, scissors, and glue
◆ pens or pencils

Activity—Part 1:
Tell the students . . . Because the people of our country have come here from all over the world, we represent many different races, cultures, languages, and religions. People, no matter where they come from, have different abilities and different types of intelligences. These differences are neither good nor bad, but they are often interesting.

Take the time, over a period of several days, if necessary, to read *The Hundred Dresses* aloud to your class. Either read it all the way through and then discuss it at the end or stop periodically while you are reading to discuss.

What is different about Wanda in the story? (She is poor, she wears only one dress, she has a somewhat unusual name, and she says she has one hundred dresses. Near the end of the story, we find out that she is also an artist.)

Activity—Part 2:
Pass out copies of page 65 and give students time to read, think, and write. (This is an activity that could be done individually, in groups, or both ways to emphasize the different learning styles in your classroom.) When everyone has completed the assignment, come together as a large group and encourage your students to share their ideas.

Activity—Part 3:
Use the paper doll on page 66 to have each student design an outfit, using a variety of materials. Have a contest like the one in *The Hundred Dresses*.

Evaluation and Processing:
Discuss the activity . . . Why do people think it is all right to make fun of other people? Why do some people think that different means funny? Are any two people really the same? One of the girls in the story was afraid that she would be teased unless she kept still. What was she afraid she would be teased about? Have you ever worn clothing that had once belonged to someone else? How did it make you feel?

Developing Respect and Empathy

I Know What You Mean: Different Is Okay

Name_____ Date _____

Directions: Read about the different kinds of intelligences. People are usually strong in one or more of the intelligence areas. Decide which intelligence areas are the strongest for Wanda and why.

Linguistic Intelligence

People with this kind of intelligence are good with words. They like to read, write, and speak.

Logical/Mathematical Intelligence

People with this kind of intelligence think like scientists. They like to figure things out and use numbers to express themselves.

Visual/Spatial Intelligence

People with this kind of intelligence think in pictures. They like to express their ideas in art such as paintings and drawings.

Bodily/Kinesthetic Intelligence

People with this kind of intelligence learn with their bodies. They like to build things and often express themselves through dance and/or sports.

Musical/Rhythmic Intelligence

People with this kind of intelligence are sensitive to sounds and rhythms. They often sing or play instruments.

Interpersonal Intelligence

People with this kind of intelligence enjoy friends and social activities. They like to work in groups.

Intrapersonal Intelligence

People with this kind of intelligence usually have deep feelings about things. They like to work alone.

I think Wanda _____

_____

_____

_____

Developing Respect and Empathy

I Know What You Mean: Different Is Okay

Directions: Use a variety of art materials to create an outfit for this paper doll. Enter your creation in a class contest similar to the one in *The Hundred Dresses*. (Do not forget to add a face and some hair too!)

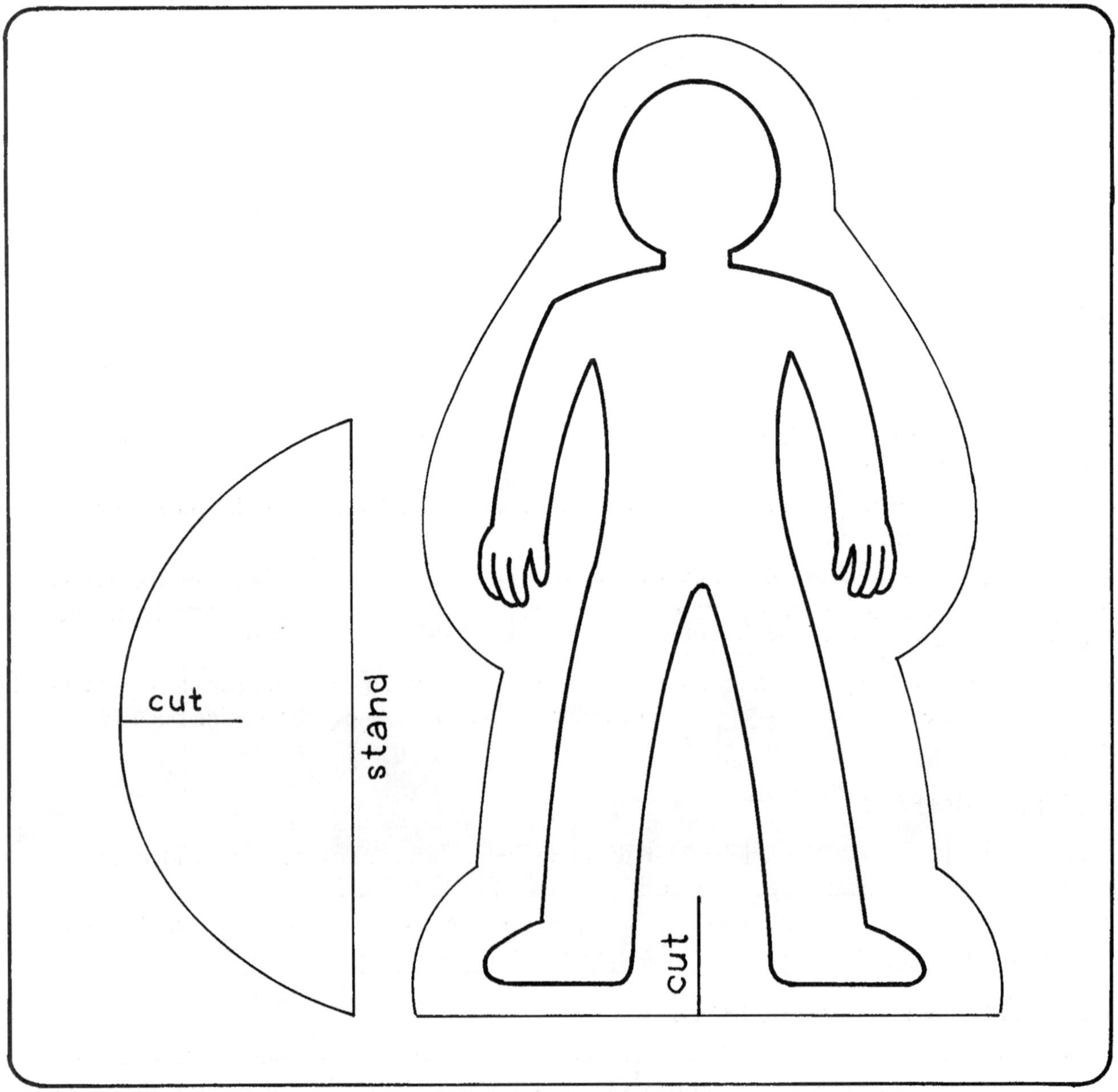

cut

stand

cut

Developing Respect and Empathy

I Know How You Feel: Different Is Okay

Purpose:

to give students an opportunity to empathize with poor children and to make an impact on poverty in their own school or neighborhood

Materials:

- ◆ *The Hundred Dresses* by Eleanor Estes (Harcourt Brace Jovanovich, 1974)
- ◆ copies of page 68, one for each student
- ◆ copies of page 69, one for each student plus one for the teacher
- ◆ copies of page 70, one for each student
- ◆ art materials
- ◆ old magazines
- ◆ pens or pencils

Activity—Part 1:

Reread *The Hundred Dresses* all the way through or just enough to refresh your students' memories about the story. Discuss the idea that many people look down on others who are poorer than they are. Why? Do kids usually have any control over their financial situations? (Note: Throughout this entire lesson be extremely sensitive to the personal financial situations of your students.)

Discuss "empathy." Have someone look up the word and read the definition to the class. How is *empathy* different from sympathy?

Pass out copies of page 68 and give students ample time to think and write. If you use the writing process, this can be a "quick write" or a first draft. Then give the students the opportunity to later do the editing and revising steps.

When the papers are completed (for your purposes), ask for volunteers to read their pieces aloud to the group. Remind the audience of good listening manners and the necessity for making positive comments.

Activity—Part 2:

Consider the ways in which you and your students can help. Food drives are often held around the holidays when people are feeling particularly generous, but people need food all year long. Organize a "Thanksgiving in_____Food Drive." (Use the suggestions on page 69 and fill in the name of any month.) Make greeting cards to go with the food. (See page 70.)

Evaluation and Processing:

Discuss the activity . . . Was our food drive a success? What could we have done to make it better? (Get donations from businesses, have more publicity, etc.) Would you like to have food drives on a regular basis?

Developing Respect and Empathy

I Know How You Feel: Different Is Okay

Name_____ Date _____

Writing Situation:

It is an unfortunate fact that some people look down on other people who are poorer than they are. We have been discussing that children who are caught in this situation usually have no control over it.

Directions for Writing:

Pretend that you are the son or daughter of poor immigrant parents. Describe your feelings when people make fun of you and your family. Try to use words that express emotions so that the reader will know how you feel.

_____

_____

_____

_____

_____

_____

_____

_____

_____

_____

_____

_____

_____

Developing Respect and Empathy

I Know How You Feel: Different Is Okay

Holiday food drives are a thoughtful way to help the poor in your community. However, people need food every day of the year, not just on the holidays. As a class, organize a food drive during an unusual time of the year. Your efforts will certainly be appreciated.

1. Ask your teacher to help you to . . .

> . . . clear your project with the principal.

> . . . communicate with your parents about the project.

> . . . find an appropriate family, group, or organization to accept your gift.

> . . . arrange to have the food picked up and delivered where it is supposed to go.

2. Make signs to let people know about your project. Be sure to include . . .

> . . . what kinds of food you are collecting (cans, jars, and other non-perishable items).

> . . . where people can donate food.

> . . . who will receive the food.

3. Follow through by . . .

> . . . being there to receive the donations and to thank people.

> . . . packaging the donations so that nothing gets broken.

> . . . having things ready to be picked up.

4. Personalize your project by . . .

> . . . making greeting cards to go with the food.

> . . . adding some gifts other than food, such as mittens, scarves, and stuffed animals for children.

> . . . tying big bows on the boxes.

Developing Respect and Empathy

I Know How You Feel: Different Is Okay

Directions: Make greeting cards by coloring, cutting, and folding the card below. Write a short message on the inside, such as "I hope you enjoy your meal!" If you would rather create your own card, fold a piece of construction paper in half and decorate it with crayons and/or markers. Cut out pictures of food from old magazines and glue them to the card.

School

From Room ____,

Be Our Guest!

cereal

CHIPS

Seventh Grade

Developing Self-Concepts

My Name: You Can Call Me . . .

Purpose:

to give students information about names in other languages and reasons people might have for wanting to anglicize their names

Materials:

- ◆ encyclopedias and other reference books
- ◆ books about names
- ◆ copies of page 73, one copy for every four students
- ◆ copies of page 74, one for each student
- ◆ laminating materials
- ◆ markers
- ◆ safety pins
- ◆ pens or pencils

Activity—Part 1:

Ask your students to do some research to find out what their names would be in other countries (for example, John would be Juan in Mexico and Sean in Ireland; Mary would be Marie in France and Maria in Mexico). Have them make name buttons (page 73) with their favorite name variations. Let them wear the buttons for a week.

Activity—Part 2:

Tell the students . . . Many people anglicize their names when they come here from other countries. To anglicize means to change to the English form or to a form that just sounds more like English. Someone named Jorge might change his name to George. Someone named Tan might change his name to Tom.

Why do you think people anglicize their names? Have you? Would you? Pass out the writing prompt on page 74 and have students follow the directions. Give them ample time to think and write. If you use the writing process, this can be a "quick write" or a first draft. Then give the students the opportunity to later do the editing and revising steps.

When the papers are completed (for your purposes), ask for volunteers to read their pieces aloud to the group. Remind the audience of good listening manners and the necessity for making positive comments. Discuss the reasons people gave. How many different reasons (pro and con) did they come up with?

Evaluation and Processing:

Discuss Part 1 of the activity . . . From what country did your chosen name for the week originate? Did you enjoy using the new name? Were you glad to return to your own name?

Discuss Part 2 of the activity . . . How many people decided that they would anglicize their names? How many decided to keep their original names?

Developing Self-Concepts

My Name: You Can Call Me . . .

Teacher Directions: Cut out a button form for each student. Ask the students to clearly print their chosen names (and countries), using a bright or dark-colored marker. Laminate the buttons. Pass out safety pins to attach the buttons to clothing.

I Am
_____
from
_____

I Am
_____
from
_____

I Am
_____
from
_____

I Am
_____
from
_____

Example:

I Am
Maria
_____
from
Spain
_____

Developing Self-Concepts

My Name: You Can Call Me . . .

Name_____ Date _____

Writing Situation:

You are a person who came to the United States from another country. You plan to stay and you are trying to decide whether or not to change your name to something that sounds more like an English language name.

Directions for Writing:

Make up the name that you would have been called in the country you came from and tell what it is. Then write about your decision. Will you change it or not? Explain the reasons for your decision. Express your thoughts clearly and in complete sentences. Try to convince the reader that you made the right decision.

_____

_____

_____

_____

_____

_____

_____

_____

_____

_____

_____

_____

_____

Developing Self-Concepts

How I Look: My Shoes Say It All

Purpose:

to give students the opportunity to explore the relationship between the shoes they wear and how they feel about themselves

Materials:

◆ shoe advertisements from newspapers and magazines

◆ copies of page 76, one for each student

◆ pens or pencils

Activity—Part 1:

Have students respond to these questions: Look at your shoes. Are you wearing sports shoes right now? Why? Do you plan to run or take part in a sport today? Are you wearing them for style and because they are in fashion? Do you wear them simply because they are comfortable? Why are shoes so important? Sketch a quick graph on the chalkboard and record your students' responses.

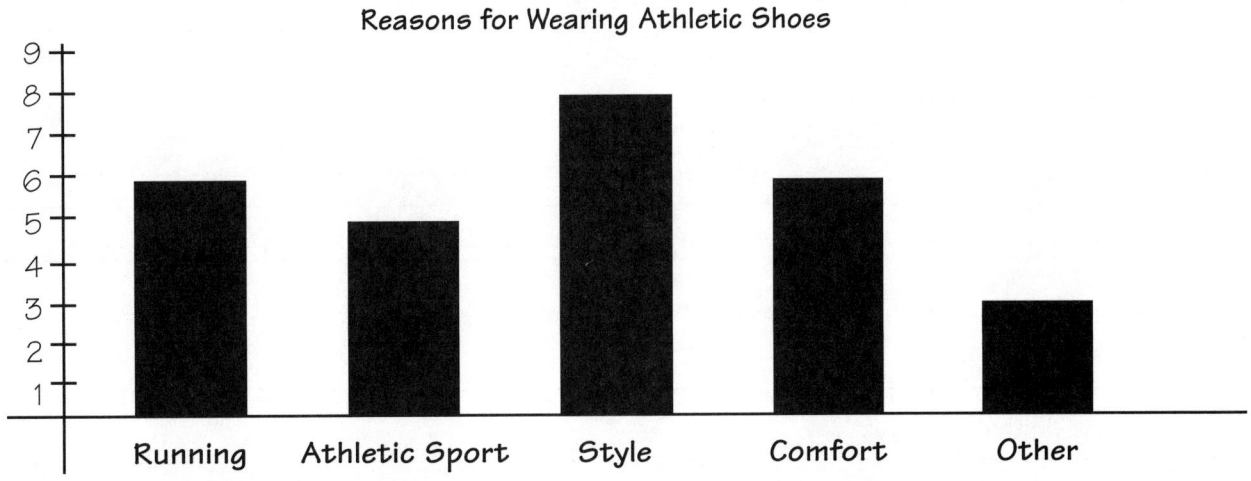

Activity—Part 2:

Pass out the questionnaire (page 76) and ask the students to fill it out. Share, compare, and discuss the completed questionnaires.

Evaluation and Processing:

Discuss with the class . . . Do you notice the shoes other people are wearing? Do you think people judge you by your shoes? Why are athletic shoes so expensive? Would they be as important if they cost a lot less? Where do you get the money to buy your shoes? If your parents pay for them, how do they feel about the high prices?

Developing Self-Concepts

How I Look: My Shoes Say It All
Shoe Questionnaire

Name_____ Date _____

Directions: Answer the questions honestly, in writing. Be prepared to discuss your answers.

1. What brand of athletic shoes do you wear?

    _____

2. What brand would you wear if you had enough money?

    _____

3. Does a sports star wear the shoes you wear? If so, who?

    _____

4. Does a sports star wear the shoes you would like to wear? If so, who?

    _____

5. Which shoe ads do you like best? Why?

    _____

    _____

6. There have been news reports that kids have stolen shoes from other kids. What could make someone do that?

    _____

    _____

    _____

    _____

    _____

    _____

Developing Self-Concepts

What I Know: Twenty Things I Would Like to Learn About

Purpose:

to give students the opportunity to think about and express some of the things that they would like to learn about

Materials:

◆ copies of page 78, one for each student

◆ copies of page 79, one copy for each invited expert

◆ pens or pencils

Activity—Part 1:

Begin this activity as a large group. Ask the students to think about the things that they would like to learn about, both at school and outside of school—things they see other people doing, things they read about, things they have seen on television, and so on. Would they like to learn a little about something or even become an expert?

Pass out the copies of "I Would Like to Learn About . . ." and give your students ample time to think while they fill it out. Encourage them to think of enough things to fill in all 20 blanks. Suggest that they might try to think of ten things to learn in school and ten things to learn outside of school. Collect the lists and put them aside for Part 2 of this activity.

Activity—Part 2:

Ask student volunteers to take turns reading their lists out loud to the class. Make a quick graph on the chalkboard (or ask a student to do it). As interests are mentioned, write them at the bottom of the graph and fill in a square above each one. If that interest or something closely related to it is mentioned again, add another square above it.

When everyone has finished reading the lists, you will probably have many interests with only one or two squares, but you may have some that were listed by many students, as shown by tall columns of squares.

Activity—Part 3:

Choose two or three of the most popular items from the chart and invite "experts" in those fields to come in and talk to your class. Use the letter on page 79 for your invitations.

Evaluation and Processing:

Discuss Part 1 of the activity . . . Were you surprised that you wanted to learn so many things? Was it hard or easy to list 20 things? Discuss Part 2 of the activity . . . Were you surprised at the things the other students listed? Did anyone else list the same things you listed?

Developing Self-Concepts

What I Know: Twenty Things I Would Like to Learn About

Name_____ Date _____

Directions: By the seventh grade you have already learned many things, but the world still has a lot to offer. Make a list of 20 things you would like to learn, either in or out of school. Would you like to learn a new craft or sport? Would you like the challenge of learning a new language or perhaps something about a period in history?

1. _____

2. _____

3. _____

4. _____

5. _____

6. _____

7. _____

8. _____

9. _____

10. _____

11. _____

12. _____

13. _____

14. _____

15. _____

16. _____

17. _____

18. _____

19. _____

20. _____

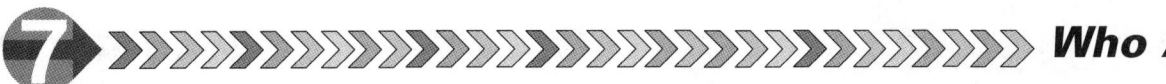

Developing Self-Concepts

What I Know: Twenty Things I Would Like to Learn About

Dear_____,

We are students in the_____grade

at_____School in_____.

Our class has been discussing things about which we would like to learn. We are

very interested in_____,

and we know that you are an expert in this field.

Our teacher suggested that we write to you to find out if you might be willing to

talk to our class. If you can come, please contact our teacher,

_____, to plan a time.

The phone number of our school is_____.

The address is   _____

                      _____

We hope you will be able to find the time to do this. Thank you for considering our invitation.

Sincerely,

_____

Developing Self-Concepts

How I Feel: Emotional Ups and Downs

Purpose:

to give students information and answer questions about the emotional ups and downs that they may be experiencing

Materials:

◆ one enlarged or overhead transparency copy of page 81, for the teacher to use as an example

◆ copies of page 82, one for each student (plus extras for continued, optional use)

◆ pens or pencils

Note: Emotional ups and downs in the seventh grade are often connected to puberty. You may want to deal with these issues as part of your regular sex education program, the parameters of which are probably mandated by your school district. However, students are often worried about their wild mood swings, and these concerns could be dealt with here as part of their developing self-concepts.

Activity—Part 1:

Say to the students . . . During the seventh grade, some people start to notice that they feel wonderful one day and terrible the next without anything really different happening to cause the changes. These feelings are called *mood swings,* and they are very common. Although they can be very uncomfortable, they do not do any harm as long as they remain as mild feelings. The only time they become a real problem is when they cause us to act in extreme ways.

Pass out the copies of page 82. Show the students how to chart their emotions by using a copy of the example on page 81. Then let the students keep track of their moods and note their circumstances and/or their actions for a day (or for a longer period if they wish).

Activity—Part 2:

After a few days, ask for student volunteers to share what they have learned about themselves, their mood swings, and their actions. Were there certain times of the day when they always felt up or down? Did they discover anything that was causing the mood swings? Were they hungry, angry, tired, etc.? Did the mood swings usually have an effect on their actions? Did acknowledging the mood swings help them to control their actions?

Evaluation and Processing:

Discuss the activity . . . How many students chose to continue charting their moods? How many students felt that the chart helped them to be aware of their moods? Did any of the students feel that the chart helped them to alter their circumstances or control their undesirable behaviors? Does self-control increase self-esteem?

Developing Self-Concepts

How I Feel: Emotional Ups and Downs

Name_____ Date _____

Directions: Carefully analyze your moods at three points during the day (morning, noon, and night). Record what you notice about your moods below.

Moods (10=Up/1=Down)	Circumstances and/or Comments

Moods (10=Up/1=Down)

10

9

8

7

6

5

4

3

2

1

Morning   Noon   Night

Circumstances and/or Comments

I went to the movies and had a great time!

Good mood—got an A on math quiz.

Really hungry—snapped at my best friend.

Developing Self-Concepts

How I Feel: Emotional Ups and Downs

Name_____ Date _____

Directions: Carefully analyze your moods at three points during the day (morning, noon, and night). Record what you notice about your moods below.

Moods (10=Up/1=Down)	Circumstances and/or Comments
10	
9	
8	
7	
6	
5	
4	
3	
2	
1	
Morning Noon Night	

Growing in Social Awareness

Names: Paper Chase

Purpose:

to give every student the opportunity to learn the names of all of the other students in the class and to associate the names with the right people

Materials:

- ◆ copies of a class list, showing last names only, one for each student
- ◆ copies of a class list, showing first names only, one for each student
- ◆ several copies of a seating chart to be used for reference
- ◆ copies of page 84, one for each student
- ◆ pens or pencils

Activity—Part 1:

This part of the activity can simply be part of your classroom management plan. Each day choose a couple of different students to pass out papers to the class. Do not give them any help. Let them quietly ask around and show papers to students until they are able to distribute all of them. If a paper has only a first or last name on it, have the student helper ask the paper's owner for the missing name. The person passing out the papers should be the one to write the missing name on the paper. The person that it belongs to can help with spelling. Rotate this job until everyone in the class has had at least one turn.

After everyone has had a turn to pass out papers, have your helpers file stacks of student papers (in portfolios, if you use them). The people doing the filing may have to ask around quietly as in the first part of the activity. Also, as above, the person filing the papers should be the one to write any missing names on the papers. Rotate this job until everyone in the class has had at least one turn. (You may want to cut down your own work by continuing this activity all year long!)

Activity—Part 2:

After everyone has had at least one turn doing each exercise of Part 1 of this activity, pass out the activity sheet on page 84 and give the students enough time to fill it out. Meet back as a large group to share and discuss the results.

Evaluation and Processing:

Test the students to see how many names they have learned. Have a contest to see who can call the most people by their correct names. Discuss the advantages of knowing the names of everyone in the class. What are the benefits? Do you enjoy having other people call you by your name? Would you say you have more friends now than you did before?

Growing in Social Awareness

Names: Paper Chase

Name_____ Date _____

1. Do any of the people in this class have the same last name?_____

   How many?_____ Write the name or names: _____

   _____

   _____

2. Do any of the people in this class have the same first name?_____

   How many?_____Write the name or names: _____

   _____

   _____

3. Look at the roll sheet listing only last names. Write in the matching first names.

   Check with people if you need to.

4. Look at the roll sheet listing only first names. Write in the matching last names.

   Check with people if you need to.

5. How many times did you need to check last names?_____

6. How many times did you need to check first names? _____

Growing in Social Awareness

Qualities: Pageant Picks

Purpose:

to encourage students to become aware of and appreciate the good qualities of their classmates

Materials:

- ◆ copies of page 86, one for each student
- ◆ copies of the class list, one for each student
- ◆ sashes made of wide ribbon or strips of construction paper
- ◆ marking pens
- ◆ pens or pencils

Activity—Part 1:

Ask your students if they have ever watched a beauty pageant on television. Ask if they have ever seen people wearing "sashes" that were awarded to them for being best in certain categories. These could be "Miss Congeniality," "Mr. Health," or "Miss Photogenic." Sometimes the sashes say things like "Most Beautiful Eyes" or "Most Talented."

Tell the students that they are going to participate in a class "Qualities Pageant" in which each person will be awarded a sash that tells his or her outstanding quality. The first step is to brainstorm qualities. Pass out copies of page 86 and have your students meet in groups to think of as many categories as they can. (They might have "Miss Congeniality" just as in a beauty pageant. They could also have "Mr. Responsibility" or "Miss Stand-Up Comedian." They could even choose categories like "Most Helpful," "Best Listener," and "Best Prepared.") Your goal should be to have more categories than there are students so that the selection process will be easy.

Post the "Sash Suggestions" around the room. After your students have had a chance to read all of the categories, pass out a class list to each student and have everybody write a category next to each name. (Tally the votes in private so that you can make any adjustments that seem appropriate.)

Activity—Part 2:

Make sashes out of ribbon or long pieces of construction paper and label them with markers. Have an awards ceremony with cookies and punch.

Evaluation and Processing:

Discuss the activity . . . Did you like your award? Do you think it suits you? Does it say anything about the way you see yourself? Does it give you a new way to think about yourself? Was it easy or hard to pick people for the different categories? When you see your classmates, do you think of the categories you picked for them? Do you think of anyone in a different way?

Growing in Social Awareness

Qualities: Pageant Picks

Name _____ Date _____

Directions: Suggest a different quality category for each strip below. Write down only positive qualities. Try not to think of any qualities of particular classmates. You will have the opportunity to match the categories to names at a later time.

Growing in Social Awareness

Similarities and Differences: Everybody Celebrates the New Year

Purpose:

to introduce students to different ways of celebrating the New Year and comparing them with contemporary American customs

Materials:

◆ *Happy New Year* by Emily Kelley (Carolrhoda Books, 1984)

◆ a large map of the world and/or a globe

◆ encyclopedias and other reference books

◆ copies of page 88, one for each student

◆ pens or pencils

Activity—Part 1:

Read *Happy New Year* aloud to your class. This short (48 pages), clearly written book contains an enormous amount of information about the way the New Year is celebrated in seven different countries: Ecuador, Iran, Japan, Israel, Vietnam, Sierra Leone, and China. It also contains bits of information about interesting celebrations in a number of other countries. Have your students find the countries on the map and/or globe as you read.

Activity—Part 2:

Ask the students . . . How is the New Year greeted in the United States? Did our celebration traditions originate here? If not, where did they come from? Pass out copies of page 88 and let your students use encyclopedias and other reference books to complete the activity sheet.

Meet back as a large group to share, compare, and discuss the results of the research done by students.

Evaluation and Processing:

Discuss the activity . . . How do you and your family celebrate the New Year? Are any of your customs (foods, ceremonies, types of gifts, religious observances) from other countries? Have your customs from other countries become part of the American celebration?

Growing in Social Awareness

Similarities and Differences: Everybody Celebrates the New Year

Name_____ Date _____

Directions: How do you celebrate the New Year? How do your friends celebrate the same holiday? Write down some of the New Year's customs that you know about. Then do some research to see if you can find out where the customs originated. Write down the results of your research in the right column.

 **Custom**	**Origin**

Growing in Social Awareness

Our Manners: As Representatives of Our School

Purpose:

to introduce the idea that a student has a responsibility to use good manners when he or she might be seen as representative of his or her school

Materials:

◆ copies of page 90, one for each student

◆ pens or pencils

Activity—Part 1:

Divide your students into groups and discuss the reasons for them, as seventh graders, to have good manners outside of school, especially when they might be seen as representatives of their school. What are good manners? Why are they important? What are the benefits of good manners outside of school? Are there any special reasons for seventh graders to have good manners outside of school?

Meet again as a large group and compare the results of the small group discussions.

Activity—Part 2:

Pass out the writing prompt (page 90). Give them ample time to think and write. If you use the writing process, this can be a "quick write" or a first draft. Then give the students the opportunity to later do the editing and revising steps.

When the papers are completed (for your purposes), ask for volunteers to read their pieces aloud to the group. Remind the audience of good listening manners and the necessity for making positive comments.

Evaluation and Processing:

Discuss the activity . . . Were any special reasons identified for seventh graders to have good manners outside of school, or were the reasons for having good manners generally the same for any grade level? Have students become more aware of their manners in dealing with people outside of school? Where and under what circumstances?

Growing in Social Awareness

Our Manners: As Representatives of Our School

Name_____ Date _____

Writing Situation:

We have been discussing reasons seventh graders should have good manners outside of school. Your small group identified some reasons and you may have additional reasons, of your own.

Directions for Writing:

Pick one or more reasons for having good manners outside of school as a seventh grader. Write about your reason(s). Explain the effects that good manners can have on you and the people around you. Express your thoughts in complete sentences.

_____

_____

_____

_____

_____

_____

_____

_____

_____

_____

_____

_____

_____

_____

Acquiring Communication Skills

Sending: I Feel . . .

Purpose:

to give students information about and practice in sending clear messages when they communicate orally, especially about conflict situations

Materials:

- ◆ copies of the fifth and sixth grade lessons on pages 24 and 25 and 56–59, a copy of each set for each student
- ◆ copies of page 92, one for each student
- ◆ dictionaries and/or thesauruses
- ◆ pens or pencils

Activity—Part 1:

Use the materials in the fifth and sixth grade lessons listed above to either introduce or reinforce your students' abilities to send *"I"* messages. Both oral and written practice will be useful.

Activity—Part 2:

Tell the students . . . The more words you know, the more clearly you will be able to communicate your feelings. You can make your *"I"* messages reflect and express your feelings more accurately by polishing and refining your use of feeling words.

Let your students use a dictionary and/or thesaurus to find synonyms for the words on page 92. Students can work alone, in partners, or in small groups. When the activity sheets are completed, meet again as a large group and discuss the differences in the definitions of the words they found.

Evaluation and Processing:

Discuss the activity . . . Were *"I"* messages new to you when you began this activity? Was it easier for you to use *"I"* messages or *"You"* messages? If you were used to using *"You"* messages, have you become better at sending *"I"* messages during the course of this activity?

Have you tried using any of the new words you looked up to express your feelings in *"I"* messages? How many synonyms were you able to find for each word given? How many words of your own did you add? How many synonyms did you find for them?

Acquiring Communication Skills

Sending: I Feel . . .

Name_____ Date _____

Directions: It is an important skill to be able to clearly communicate the way you feel, especially during a conflict situation. Find at least three synonyms for each of the words below. Write the synonyms on the short lines below the original words. Then write a short definition for each word on the right side. Please use a dictionary or a thesaurus for help and use the back of this paper if you need more space.

angry

_____   _____

_____   _____

_____   _____

sad

_____   _____

_____   _____

_____   _____

happy

_____   _____

_____   _____

_____   _____

surprised

_____   _____

_____   _____

_____   _____

Acquiring Communication Skills

Receiving: I Hear . . .

Purpose:

to give students information about and practice in active listening in order to enhance the communication process

Materials:

- ◆ copies of the fifth and sixth grade lessons on pages 26 and 27, and 60 and 61, a copy of each set for each student
- ◆ a copy of page 94, one for each pair of students
- ◆ scissors
- ◆ pens or pencils

Activity—Part 1:

Use the materials in the fifth and sixth grade lessons listed above to either introduce active listening or reinforce your students' abilities to listen actively. It is helpful to have a great deal of practice in this formula kind of active listening before moving on to more casual statements.

Activity—Part 2:

Tell the students . . . Once you know the formula for active listening and can restate the information to show that you understand what was sent, you are ready for more casual statements of active listening, such as

> I hear that you are upset . . .
>
> I can sense that you are angry . . .
>
> It is evident that you felt really surprised . . .
>
> I think I understand now. You feel . . .

Divide your students into pairs. Give each pair of students a copy of page 94. Tell the students to cut the paper into strips and to try not to read the strips as they do so. Then, have them place the strips in a hat, bag, box, or some other item from which they can be drawn. Have your students role-play some situations, using non-formula active listening to respond to *"I"* messages. One person will draw a slip of paper and read the *"I"* message aloud. The other person will answer extemporaneously with an active listening statement. Then the students will switch roles and repeat the process.

Evaluation and Processing:

Discuss the activity . . . Would you rather use the active listening formula or make up a more casual answer? Which is easier for you? Which is more effective? Why do you think so?

Has anyone in this class given you an answer that showed active listening? What did he or she say? What was your original *"I"* message?

Acquiring Communication Skills

Receiving: I Hear . . .

Teacher Directions: The blank strips at the bottom of this page are available for you to add some scenarios which might be particularly familiar to your own classroom situation. Give a copy of this page to each pair of students. Tell them to cut out the strips and then participate in some role-playing exercises as described on page 93.

I hate having my desk messed up. I want you to move your books.
I feel happy when you are polite. I wish you were polite all of the time.
I was disappointed when you didn't call me with the homework assignment. I would like you to be dependable.
I'm upset that you have to take the bus today. I wanted you to come over to my house after school.
I was shocked to find out that you told a lie. I want you to be honest.
I feel angry when I hear you call people names. I want you to be kind.

Acquiring Communication Skills

Responding: I Can . . .

Purpose:

to give students information about and practice in using a variety of listening responses

Materials:

- ◆ copies of the fifth and sixth grade lessons on pages 28–31 and 62 and 63, a copy of each set for each student
- ◆ pens or pencils

Activity—Part 1:

Use the materials in the fifth and sixth grade lessons listed above to either introduce or reinforce your students' abilities to respond appropriately to information that they are given orally.

Activity—Part 2:

Tell the students . . . There is still another response for communications that are sent in *"I"* messages and received through active listening. It is the response that gives information about how the situation looks from the other person's perspective. Here is an example:

- ◆ *First Person* (*"I" Message*)—I was disappointed when you didn't call me with the homework assignment. I would like you to be dependable.

- ◆ *Second Person* (*Active Listening*)—I can hear that you feel like I let you down about the homework assignment. You were depending on me.

- ◆ *Second Person* (*Another Perspective*)—Can I tell you how it looks from my side? (At this point the listener may give an *"I"* message, and the whole process starts again.)

Repeat the *"I"* messages from the preceding activity (or any of the activities), extending each situation with a look at the listener's perspective.

Evaluation and Processing:

Discuss . . . Are you now able to (1) give a clear *"I"* message, (2) listen actively, and (3) respond from your own perspective with another *"I"* message? Depending on the circumstances, you may need to be able to do all of these things in order to communicate effectively.

Developing Respect and Empathy

I Know What You Mean: Cultural Heritage

Purpose:

to give students the experience (through literature) of immigrants' attachments to their cultural heritages

Materials:

- *Hello, My Name Is Scrambled Eggs* by Jamie Gilson (Simon & Schuster, 1986)
- copies of page 97, one for each student
- copies of page 98, one for each student
- copies of page 99, one for each student

- encyclopedias and other resource books for studying immigration
- writing paper
- calculators
- pens or pencils

Activity—Part 1:

Read aloud, or have the students read, *Hello, My Name Is Scrambled Eggs*, a few chapters at a time, over the span of a week. Discuss the events in the book as you go along.

Discuss idioms. Idioms are a type of figurative language. They are not easily translated from one language to another. The English language has many idioms which make it hard for people to learn English. Here are some examples:

- She made my blood boil. (She made me very angry.)
- He is bouncing off the walls. (He is very active.)
- They are going downhill with the brakes off. (They are out of control.)
- I could eat a horse. (I am really hungry.)

Pass out copies of page 97 and have your students work in partners to complete the assignment. Meet as a large group to compare and discuss their results.

Activity—Part 2:

This country has experienced many waves of immigration. Have the students work in groups or in pairs to complete page 98. Meet back as a large group to compare graphs and answers.

Activity—Part 3:

Read chapter two, "My Cousin" out loud. Ask your students to complete the activity on page 99. Compare and discuss their answers.

Evaluation and Processing:

Discuss . . . What is one reason that it is hard for people to learn to speak English? What other languages do members of this class speak? Can anyone give us an example of an idiom in another language? Can you translate it into English? What does it mean in the other language?

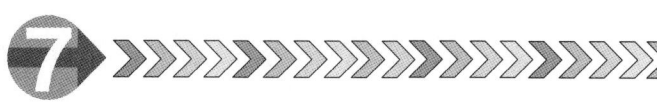

Developing Respect and Empathy

I Know What You Mean: Cultural Heritage

Before Tuan and his family arrived, Jeff Zito, the minister, talked to everyone about how to treat them. He told them not to shake hands, motion for them to come with a hand, or use sayings they will not understand, like "stick with me" or "hit the books."

These sayings are called idioms. *Idioms* are phrases that mean something other than the literal translation. For example, when Harvey said he would "show Tuan the ropes," he did not really mean he was going to show him some ropes; he meant he would show him how things are done.

Below are some idioms commonly used in the English language. Working with a partner, use a piece of paper to write down how you would explain these idioms to someone who is not fluent in English.

Don't let the cat out of the bag.

She's full of hot air.

He's got a big head.

Hit the road.

You're in the doghouse.

Hold your horses.

I woke up on the wrong side of the bed.

She's talking out of both sides of her mouth.

It goes in one ear and out the other.

Don't spill the beans.

He has a green thumb.

She's making a mountain out of a molehill.

I'm all ears.

I've got butterflies in my stomach.

He has a heart of gold.

Keep it under your hat.

Put a lid on it.

Let's put our heads together.

It's a drop in the bucket.

I'm all thumbs.

He has two left feet.

Keep a stiff upper lip.

He has to pay through the nose.

I have to bring home the bacon.

Don't throw out the baby with the bathwater.

Developing Respect and Empathy

I Know What You Mean: Cultural Heritage

An immigrant is a person who has left his or her homeland and moved to a different country to live. Immigrants have many reasons for moving from country to country. Some of the major causes of immigration are: to find better jobs; to seek a better way of life; to escape persecution, war, starvation, and/or disease.

Use encyclopedias and other resource books to research the countries listed in the chart below and to find out the reasons why each group came to the United States. Use the data from the chart to make a bar graph showing the number of immigrants from each country listed. Above each bar, write the years in which the group experienced the greatest wave of immigration.

Complete the questions at the bottom of the page.

Immigrants	Years of Major Immigration	Approximate Number of Immigrants
Irish	1840s and 1850s	1 ½ million
Germans	1840s to 1880s	4 million
Poles	1880s to 1920s	1 million
Jews	1880s to 1920s	2 ½ million
Mexicans	1910s and 1920s	700,000
Dominicans, Haitians, & Jamaicans	1970s and 1980s	900,000
Vietnamese	1970s and 1980s	500,000

Use the data above and your bar graph to solve the following problems. You may want to use a calculator.

1. How many immigrants are represented in the chart? _____

   Round your answer to the nearest million. _____
   Use the rounded answer to complete problem 2.

2. What percentage of the total number of immigrants came from each of the following groups:

   a. Poles? _____

   b. Mexicans? _____

   c. Vietnamese? _____

3. What percentage of the total immigrant population represented in the chart arrived in the 1970s and 1980s? _____

98

Developing Respect and Empathy

I Know What You Mean: Cultural Heritage

Name_____ Date _____

Directions: After reading the second chapter, "My Cousin" answer the following questions.

1. Why did the author's cousin live with the author's family?

   _____

   _____

2. Were the author and his cousin the same age?

   _____

   _____

3. Describe how the author's cousin tamed and trained the three wild birds.

   _____

   _____

4. What trick did the cousin use to catch his python?

   _____

   _____

5. What happened when the two boys rested on a fallen "tree"?

   _____

   _____

   _____

6. Although the author's cousin did not want to go to school, he knew more than anybody about one thing. What was it?

   _____

   _____

Developing Respect and Empathy

I Know How You Feel: Cultural Heritage

Purpose:

to give students the experience (through literature) of immigrants' attachments to their cultural heritages

Materials:

- ◆ *Hello, My Name Is Scrambled Eggs* by Jamie Gilson (Simon & Schuster, 1986)
- ◆ *The Land I Lost: Adventures of a Boy in Vietnam* by Huynh Quang Nhuong (Harper Trophy, 1982)
- ◆ copies of page 101, one for each student
- ◆ copies of page 102, one for each student
- ◆ copies of page 103, one for each student
- ◆ pens or pencils

Activity—Part 1:

Remind your students of how Harvey tried to turn Tuan into an American in *Hello, My Name Is Scrambled Eggs*. Pass out copies of page 101 and give your students ample time to think and write. If you use the writing process, this can be a "quick write" or a first draft. Then give the students the opportunity to later do the editing and revising steps.

When the papers are completed (for your purposes), ask for volunteers to read their pieces aloud to the group. Remind the audience of good listening manners and the necessity for making positive comments. Discuss the feelings they identified.

Activity—Part 2:

Have the students read *The Land I Lost: Adventures of a Boy in Vietnam*. After everyone has read the book, read a few chapters out loud. Discuss the events.

Read the introduction, "The Land I Lost," aloud to the class. Discuss. Then pass out copies of page 102 and give your students plenty of time to draw and write. Display the results on a bulletin board for everyone to enjoy.

Evaluation and Processing:

Ask the students . . . Even though many people have had to leave their countries because of war or persecution, they may still have deep feelings about the places in which they were born or grew up. Why? If you have had this experience, could you share your feelings with the class? If you have not had this experience, what feelings do you think you would have if you had to leave your country? Is anger an appropriate feeling to have? sadness? joy? Should anyone try to decide if another person's feelings are the right ones?

Developing Respect and Empathy

I Know How You Feel: Cultural Heritage

Name_____ Date _____

Writing Situation:

We have been discussing how Harvey tried to turn Tuan into an American in *Hello, My Name Is Scrambled Eggs*. He even tried to change Tuan's name to Tom. How did Tuan feel about this?

Directions for Writing:

Pretend that you are Tuan. You do not understand much of what is being said to you or about you. How do you feel when Harvey changes your name? Write about the feelings that you (Tuan) have. Try to use words that express emotions so that the reader will know how you feel.

_____

_____

_____

_____

_____

_____

_____

_____

_____

_____

_____

_____

_____

_____

Developing Respect and Empathy

I Know How You Feel: Cultural Heritage

Name_____ Date _____

Directions: Pretend that you are the author of the book *The Land I Lost: Adventures of a Boy in Vietnam*. In the box, draw a picture that you think he would choose to remind him of his country. Explain why you chose this picture on the lines at the bottom of the page.

_____

_____

_____

_____

 **Why Should We Care?**

Developing Respect and Empathy

I Know How You Feel: *Cultural Heritage*

Name_____ Date _____

Directions: Pretend that you are leaving your own country. In the box below, draw a picture to remind you of the things you love the best about your homeland. Explain why you chose the things that you included in your picture on the lines at the bottom of the page.

_____

_____

_____

_____

_____

Eighth Grade

Developing Self-Concepts

My Name: Name-Calling

Purpose:

to give students information about name-calling and reasons for avoiding its practice

Materials:

- ◆ encyclopedias and other reference materials
- ◆ an enlarged copy of page 106
- ◆ poster paper
- ◆ markers

Activity—Part 1:

Tell the students . . . People today are very aware of name-calling. Not too many years ago, people often ignored name-calling. In addition to calling people names, it was common to use the same names when talking about certain groups of people. Stand-up comedians did it a lot. Certain names always got a laugh.

Even though it hurt their feelings just as much then as it does today, people were expected to be good sports about the more good-natured names and just ignore the really mean ones. Not anymore! Name-calling is considered harassment and is often dealt with legally.

Nevertheless, some people still try to get away with it. Today, some name-callers might be less likely to call someone a name that might be considered a racial, ethnic, or religious slur, but they may still try to get away with terms that insult others on physical grounds. They might use a word that is a comment about age, appearance, or some physical limitation.

Have you ever been called a name you did not like? What did you do? What should you do if it ever happens? Discuss.

Have you ever called other people names? What is the best way to tell if a name is appropriate or not? Discuss.

Activity—Part 2:

Post an enlarged copy of page 106 in the classroom. Divide your students into groups to work on making up catchy slogans of their own. Share, discuss, and polish the resulting slogans. Ask them to write the slogans in large letters on long strips of paper to post around the room (and even the school).

Evaluation and Processing:

Discuss the activity . . . Is name-calling a problem in this school? In this classroom? Is it less of a problem now? Have the slogans been helpful in reminding you not to call people inappropriate names?

Developing Self-Concepts

My Name: *Name-Calling*

Teacher Directions: Make a classroom poster by enlarging this simple symbol and reminder.

NAME-CALLING

Developing Self-Concepts

How I Look: Uniforms—Yes or No?

Purpose:

to gather information about and discuss the current trend of uniforms for public school students

Materials:

- ◆ copies of page 108, one for each student
- ◆ pens or pencils

Activity—Part 1:

Tell the students . . . Students in most private schools have usually worn uniforms. Now there is a movement in many places to have the students in public schools wear uniforms also. What do you think of this idea?

Pass out copies of the page 108 and have your students brainstorm ideas in groups, with partners, or as individuals. Let them complete the activity sheets by writing their own personal opinions.

Activity—Part 2:

Meet as a large group to compare points for and against school uniforms. List the points for and against on the chalkboard. Compare and discuss.

Then ask for volunteers to read their personal opinion statements. Discuss the effects of uniforms on self-concepts. Do people feel differently about themselves when they are wearing uniforms? Do they feel more or less responsible for their own behavior? Why?

Ask the students . . . If you had to wear a uniform, what would be acceptable to you? Take a minute or two to think about it and then describe the uniform you could live with. (If your students already wear uniforms, ask them if there is anything that they would like to change about their uniforms.)

Evaluation and Processing:

Be on the lookout for current newspaper and magazine articles about uniforms in schools. Post them in the classroom and discuss. Does this new information cause anyone to change his or her original opinion about uniforms?

Developing Self-Concepts

How I Look: Uniforms—Yes or No?

Name_____ Date _____

List five points in favor of school uniforms.	List five points against school uniforms.
•	•
•	•
•	•
•	•
•	•

What are your personal opinions about school uniforms? _____

_____

_____

_____

_____

Developing Self-Concepts

What I Know: I Need to Know More

Purpose:

to give students the opportunity to acquire information about what they need to know for high school

Materials:

- ◆ copies of page 110, one for each student
- ◆ pens or pencils

Activity—Part 1:

Prepare for this activity by contacting the student leadership organization at your local high school. Ask them if they might provide a speaker to give your students information and answer questions about what they need to know to be successful in high school. Arrange a time and help your students to prepare questions for the speaker.

Tell the students . . . Life is much easier when we have all of the information we need. This is especially true during a time of transition such as the move from middle school (or junior high school) to high school. I have invited a representative from the high school to come and talk to you and answer your questions. You can work in groups to discuss and write down the questions you would like to ask the speaker.

Pass out copies of page 110 and have your students work in groups to formulate questions. Ask them to assign questions to group members and have them read the questions to you for practice. (This will also give you a chance to preview the questions for content.)

Tell the students that they will also be responsible for writing down the answers to the questions that their group asks.

Activity—Part 2:

Conduct the question-and-answer session with the high school student representative. Note the answers to the questions yourself so that you can compare information with your students after the session. When the session is over, have your students discuss the results.

Ask each group to rewrite their questions and the given answers on fresh forms. Insert these into a three-ring binder for easy reference in your classroom.

Have the class collaborate on a thank-you note to be sent to the visiting high school student representative.

Evaluation and Processing:

Discuss the activity . . . Were your questions answered to your satisfaction? Do you know more about high school now? How did getting this information make you feel?

Developing Self-Concepts

What I Know: I Need to Know More

Student _____ Group _____

Directions: Think of three questions that you have about high school. Write them below.

Question #1: _____

_____

Answer: _____

_____

_____

Question #2: _____

_____

Answer: _____

_____

_____

Question #3: _____

_____

Answer: _____

_____

_____

Developing Self-Concepts

How I Feel: I Feel with My . . .

Purpose:

to give students the opportunity to express and analyze their emotions

Materials:

- ◆ copies of page 112, one for each student
- ◆ pens or pencils
- ◆ assorted art materials

Activity—Part 1:

Tell the students . . . Have you ever asked someone, "How do you feel?" and they responded, "I feel with my hands"? It probably was not the answer you were expecting, but it was certainly true. In fact, we feel with all of our senses. We feel with our eyes (we see beautiful or horrible things). We feel with our ears (we hear sounds that make us feel really good or really awful). Similarly, our senses of smell, taste, and touch also make us feel.

Pass out copies of page 112 and have each student complete it. Then meet as a large group to share, compare, and discuss the results.

Activity—Part 2:

Explain to your students that feelings are often hard to express in words, but there are many other methods to express the ways we feel. Have your students choose one or more of the feeling statements they made on the activity sheets to interpret through another medium—a drawing, a painting, a mobile, a melody, a series of movements, etc. Ask for volunteers to share their expressions with the class.

Evaluation and Processing:

Discuss the activity . . . Is it easy for you to express your feelings in words, or does expression in another medium come easier to you? Which one?

(This would be a perfect time to teach students about the multiple intelligences. It is important for students to recognize that there are a number of ways of thinking. For a quick overview of the intelligences, refer to the lesson starting on page 64 of this book. Also, Teacher Created Materials, Inc. has published a book entitled *Multiple Intelligences Activities.*)

Developing Self-Concepts

How I Feel: I Feel With My . . .

Name_____ Date _____

Directions: Our senses cause us to feel many emotions. Describe below five ways your senses make you feel.

I feel_____when I see _____

_____

_____

I feel_____when I hear_____

_____

_____

I feel_____when I smell_____

_____

_____

I feel_____when I taste _____

_____

_____

I feel_____when I touch _____

_____

_____

Growing in Social Awareness

Names: Party Games

Purpose:

to give every student the opportunity to learn the names of all the other students in the class and to associate the names with the right people

Materials:

◆ copies of the class roster to be used for reference

◆ copies of page 114, one for each student

◆ pens or pencils

Activity—Part 1:

Have a name party and play any icebreaker games that you can think of. One good party game is "Name Clues." Pass out copies of page 114 and have your students each write four clues to their own names. Decide if you will use last names or first names ahead of time. The hardest clue should be the first and the easiest clue should be the last.

Examples: My name sounds like something that grows in the woods. (*Pyne*)
Look for me where Santa Claus lives. (*North*)
People might think they can walk all over me. (*Street*)
Is this city really yellow? (*Amarillo*)
Starts with "R" and ends with "Z." (*Ramirez*)

Have your students tape their first clues to the fronts of their clothes and let everyone circulate around the room. When someone thinks he or she has identified a name, check. If the identification is correct, take the clue and write the names of the person identified and the person who made the identification on it and lay it aside. Have the person identified give you the rest of his or her clues too and clip them together with the first one. Everyone keeps circulating. Call time after about 10 minutes and have people whose names still have not been guessed take off their first clues and put on their second ones. Repeat until all of the clues have been used or until all of the names have been guessed. The winners will be the people who identified the hardest clues and the people who were identified last or not at all. Make up your own variations for additional fun and exposure to names.

Activity—Part 2:

This part of the activity can simply be part of your classroom management plan. Choose one or more suggestions from the lessons on pages 14 and 15, 48 and 49, and 83 and 84 of this book to help your students become familiar with one another's names.

Evaluation and Processing:

Test the students on the names they know. Have a contest to see who can call the most people by their correct names. Discuss the advantages of knowing the names of everyone in the class. What are the benefits? Do you enjoy having other people call you by your name? Would you say you have more friends now than you did before?

8 >>>>>>>>>>>>>>>>>>>>>>>>>> *Who Are You?*

Growing in Social Awareness

Names: Party Games

Name_____   Date _____

Directions: Write one clue about your name on each of the clue strips below. Then cut them apart.
Clue number one should be the hardest and clue number four should be the easiest.

Clue

1

Clue

2

Clue

3

Clue

4

Growing in Social Awareness

Qualities: Yearbook Biographies

Purpose:

to give students the opportunity to learn and write short biographies of other members of the class

Materials:

- ◆ copies of page 116, one for each student
- ◆ copies of page 117, one for each student
- ◆ scratch paper
- ◆ pens or pencils
- ◆ one three-ring binder for the class book
- ◆ folders for student yearbooks, one for each student
- ◆ individual pictures of students
- ◆ hole punch
- ◆ tape or glue
- ◆ camera and film

Activity—Part 1:

Have your students create the material for a class yearbook by interviewing each other and writing yearbook biographies.

Pass out copies of page 116 to each student. Partners can interview each other, or you can have your students draw names of people to interview.

When the interviews have been completed, have each student write a short biography based on the information gathered. Have them do this on scratch paper so that the pieces can go through an editing process before being copied onto page 117.

You or a student can complete the project by adding a picture of each student (a couple of rolls of film should suffice), punching the pages, and putting the book together.

Activity—Part 2:

Turn this into a really meaningful activity by making a copy of the classroom yearbook for each student in your class to have for a keepsake of the last year in junior high or middle school.

Take time to read through the whole book as a group. Compare birthplaces, languages spoken, length of time in your school, favorite subjects and activities, and so on.

Evaluation and Processing:

Discuss the activity . . . What was the best part of this activity? What was the most fun? What aspects of the activity seemed to be the easiest and the hardest? Do you feel that you know your classmates better? Are you glad to have a copy of your own to remember this year by?

Growing in Social Awareness

Qualities: Yearbook Biographies

Directions: Ask your partner the following questions and write down his or her answers. Use the back of this page if you need more space.

Questionnaire

Name of Person Being Interviewed _____

Name of Interviewer _____

1. Where were you born? _____

2. What languages do you speak? _____

3. How long have you attended this school? _____

4. What school did you attend before this one? _____

   _____

5. What are your favorite school subjects? _____

6. What activities do you take part in? _____

7. What sports do you like? _____

   _____

8. What is the most exciting experience you have ever had? _____

   _____

   _____

9. What career plans do you have? _____

   _____

Growing in Social Awareness

Qualities: Yearbook Biographies

Directions: Use the information that you learned during your interview to write a short biography. Use the back of this page if you need more writing space.

(picture)

_____
(name)

_____

_____

_____

_____

_____

_____

Growing in Social Awareness

Similarities and Differences: We All Came from Somewhere Else

Purpose:

to introduce and/or reinforce the concept that all Americans are either immigrants or the descendants of immigrants

Materials:

- ◆ *Ellis Island: New Hope in a New Land* by William Jay Jacobs (Macmillan Child Group, 1990)
- ◆ large world map and/or globe
- ◆ copies of page 119, one for each student
- ◆ pens or pencils

Activity—Part 1:

Read *Ellis Island: New Hope in a New Land* aloud to your class and discuss the information as you go along. It is a short book (34 pages), and it will lend itself to an in-depth discussion over a period of a day or two.

Activity—Part 2:

Point out to your students that everyone in the United States (in fact, in both North and South America) came here from somewhere else. Even the people who are now called Native Americans came here from somewhere else. Scientists think that they came over a land bridge from Asia when a great deal of water was frozen in glaciers, thus lowering the ocean level. (Point this area out on the map and/or globe.)

Make a sketch (like a family tree) on the chalkboard and fill it in, using your own information. On each line write the places the people came from instead of names. Start at the bottom of the board with your own country and branch up to the countries from which your mother and father came and so on.

_____	_____		_____	_____
grandmother	grandfather		grandmother	grandfather

	_____		_____	
	mother		father	

_____
my country

Pass out the copies of page 119. Tell your students to take this activity home so that their families may help them. Explain that they, or their family helpers, can add more lines to the chart as needed.

Evaluation and Processing:

When your students return their charts, encourage them to share what they learned and then post the charts on a bulletin board. Have them locate the countries on the world map.

Growing in Social Awareness

Similarities and Differences: We All Came from Somewhere Else

Name _____ Date _____

Directions: Fill in the names of the countries from which your family members came. (You do not need to include the people's names.)

great grandfather
_____
_____

great grandmother

great grandfather
_____
_____

great grandmother

great grandfather
_____
_____

great grandmother

great grandfather
_____
_____

great grandmother

_____   _____
grandmother   grandfather

_____   _____
grandmother   grandfather

_____
mother

_____
father

_____
my country

Growing in Social Awareness

Our Manners: As Teenagers

Purpose:

to introduce and/or reinforce the idea that teenagers have a special responsibility to use good manners

Materials:

- ◆ copies of page 121, one for each student
- ◆ pens or pencils

Activity—Part 1:

Divide your students into groups to discuss the reasons teenagers need to have good manners: What are good teenage manners? Why are they important? What are the benefits of good manners for teenagers? Are there any special reasons for teenagers to have good manners?

Meet as a large group and compare the results of the small group discussions.

Activity—Part 2:

Pass out copies of the writing prompt (page 121). Give your students ample time to think and write. If you use the writing process, this can be a "quick write" or a first draft. Then give the students the opportunity to later do the editing and revising steps.

When the papers are completed (for your purposes), ask for volunteers to read their pieces aloud to the group. Remind the audience of good listening manners and the necessity for making positive comments.

Evaluation and Processing:

Discuss the activity . . . Were any of the reasons for having good manners particularly important for teenagers? Were the reasons for having good manners generally the same for any age group? Have students become more aware of their manners in dealing with people in general?

Has there been any positive feedback about the manners of students in your class? (Sometimes, people are so surprised when they meet a teenager with good manners that they will take the time to call the school or even the newspaper.)

Growing in Social Awareness

Our Manners: As Teenagers

Manners for Teenagers

Name_____ Date _____

Writing Situation:

We have been discussing some of the reasons teenagers need to have good manners. Your small group identified some reasons, and you may have additional reasons of your own.

Directions for Writing:

Pick one (or more) of the reasons that teenagers should have good manners and write about it (or them). Explain the effects that good manners have on you and the people around you. Express your thoughts in complete sentences.

_____

_____

_____

_____

_____

_____

_____

_____

_____

_____

_____

_____

_____

_____

Acquiring Communication Skills

Sending: I Feel . . .

Purpose:

to give students information about and practice in sending clear messages when they communicate orally, especially about a conflict situation

Materials:

◆ copies of the fifth, sixth, and seventh grade lessons on pages 24 and 25, 56–59, and 91 and 92, a copy of each set for each student

◆ pens or pencils

Activity—Part 1:

Use any or all of the materials in the lessons listed above to either introduce or reinforce your students' abilities to send *"I"* messages. Both oral and written practice will be useful.

Activity—Part 2:

After your students have had an opportunity to practice their sending skills through the use of the materials, let them pass on their skills to other students. Invite another class to your room to be the students and encourage the members of your class to plan some lessons to teach them.

You can have the students teach in pairs or have a small group of your students teach a small group of visiting students. Whichever way you choose, have everyone meet in a large group at the end of each lesson to demonstrate what they have learned.

The visiting students will benefit from learning about *"I"* messages and your students will internalize what they have learned on a deeper level by teaching it to others.

Evaluation and Processing:

Discuss the activity . . . Did you enjoy teaching about *"I"* message, communication to the other students? Was it harder to learn it yourself or to teach it to someone else? What did you learn from the teaching process? Did you encounter any problems? What were they? Did you meet with success? Explain.

Acquiring Communication Skills

Receiving: I Hear . . .

Purpose:

to give students information about and practice in active listening in order to enhance the communication process

Materials:

◆ copies of the fifth, sixth, and seventh grade lessons on pages 26 and 27, 60 and 61, and 93 and 94, a copy of each set for each student

◆ pens or pencils

Activity—Part 1:

Use any or all of the materials from the lessons listed above to either introduce or reinforce your students' abilities to use the techniques of active listening.

Activity—Part 2:

After your students have had an opportunity to practice their receiving skills through the use of the materials, let them pass on their skills to other students. Invite another class to your room to be the students and encourage the members of your class to plan some lessons to teach them.

You can have the students teach in pairs or have a small group of your students teach a small group of visiting students. Whichever way you choose, have everyone meet in a large group at the end of each lesson to demonstrate what they have learned.

The visiting students will benefit from learning, about active listening and your students will internalize what they have learned on a deeper level by teaching it to others.

Evaluation and Processing:

Discuss the activity . . . Did you enjoy teaching active listening to other students? Was it harder to learn it yourself or to teach it to someone else? Which was harder to teach—how to send *"I"* messages or how to use active listening techniques? What did you learn from the teaching process? Did you encounter any problems? What were they? Were you able to overcome the problems? Explain.

 >>>>>>>>>>>>>>>>>>>>>>>>>>>>>>> *Can We Talk?*

Acquiring Communication Skills

Responding: I Can . . .

Purpose:

to give students information about and practice in using a variety of listening responses

Materials:

◆ copies of the fifth, sixth, and seventh grade lessons on pages 28–31, 62 and 63, and 95, a copy of each set for each student

◆ pens or pencils

Activity—Part 1:

Use any or all of the materials in the lessons listed above to either introduce or reinforce your students' abilities to respond appropriately to oral communication.

Activity—Part 2:

After your students have had an opportunity to practice their responding skills through the use of the materials, let them pass on their skills to other students. Invite another class to be the students and encourage the members of your class to plan some lessons to teach them.

You can have the students teach in pairs or have a small group of your students teach a small group of visiting students. Whichever way you choose, have everyone meet in a large group at the end of each lesson to demonstrate what they have learned.

The visiting students will benefit from learning about oral communication, and your students will internalize what they have learned on a deeper level by teaching it to others.

Evaluation and Processing:

Discuss the activity . . . Did you enjoy teaching other students how to respond to oral communication? Was it harder to learn it yourself or to teach it to someone else? Which was hardest to teach—how to send *"I"* messages, how to use active listening techniques, or how to respond to oral communications? What did you learn from the teaching process? Did you encounter any problems? What were they? Were you able to overcome the problems? Explain.

Developing Respect and Empathy

I Know What You Mean: Death and Remembrance

Purpose:

to give students the opportunity to experience (within the safety of literature) respect and empathy for someone who is dying or someone who is grieving

Materials:

- ◆ encyclopedias and other reference books
- ◆ a large world map and/or globe
- ◆ *Sadako and the Thousand Paper Cranes* by Eleanor Coerr (Dell, 1979)
- ◆ copies of page 126, one for each student
- ◆ copies of page 127, one for each student
- ◆ copies of page 128, one for each student
- ◆ pens or pencils

Activity—Part 1:

Read *Sadako and the Thousand Paper Cranes* aloud to your class. Do not forget to read the prologue and the epilogue. Pass out copies of page 126 and have your students answer the questions. Compare and discuss their answers.

Activity—Part 2:

Pass out copies of page 127. Discuss the location of Hiroshima. Tell your students to use reference books to answer the questions on page 128. Meet as a large group to compare and discuss their answers.

Evaluation and Processing:

Ask the students . . . Do people today feel confident that dropping the atomic bomb was the right thing to do? How did people feel at the time? Did they know what the results would be? One of the results of the atomic bomb was the Cold War. What was the Cold War? When did it end?

Developing Respect and Empathy

I Know What You Mean: Death and Remembrance

Name_____ Date _____

Directions: After reading *Sadako and the Thousand Paper Cranes,* answer the questions below. Use the back side of this paper if you need more writing space.

1. Was Sadako a real person? _____

2. Where did she live? _____

_____

3. When did she live? _____

4. What is Peace Day? _____

_____

5. How is Peace Day celebrated? _____

_____

6. What was Sadako's secret? _____

_____

7. What did the tests in the hospital show? _____

_____

8. What is the legend of the thousand paper cranes? _____

_____

_____

9. How has Sadako been remembered by the children of Japan?_____

_____

_____

Developing Respect and Empathy

I Know What You Mean: Death and Remembrance

Directions: Use a world map or a globe to find Hiroshima. Mark Hiroshima on the map below.

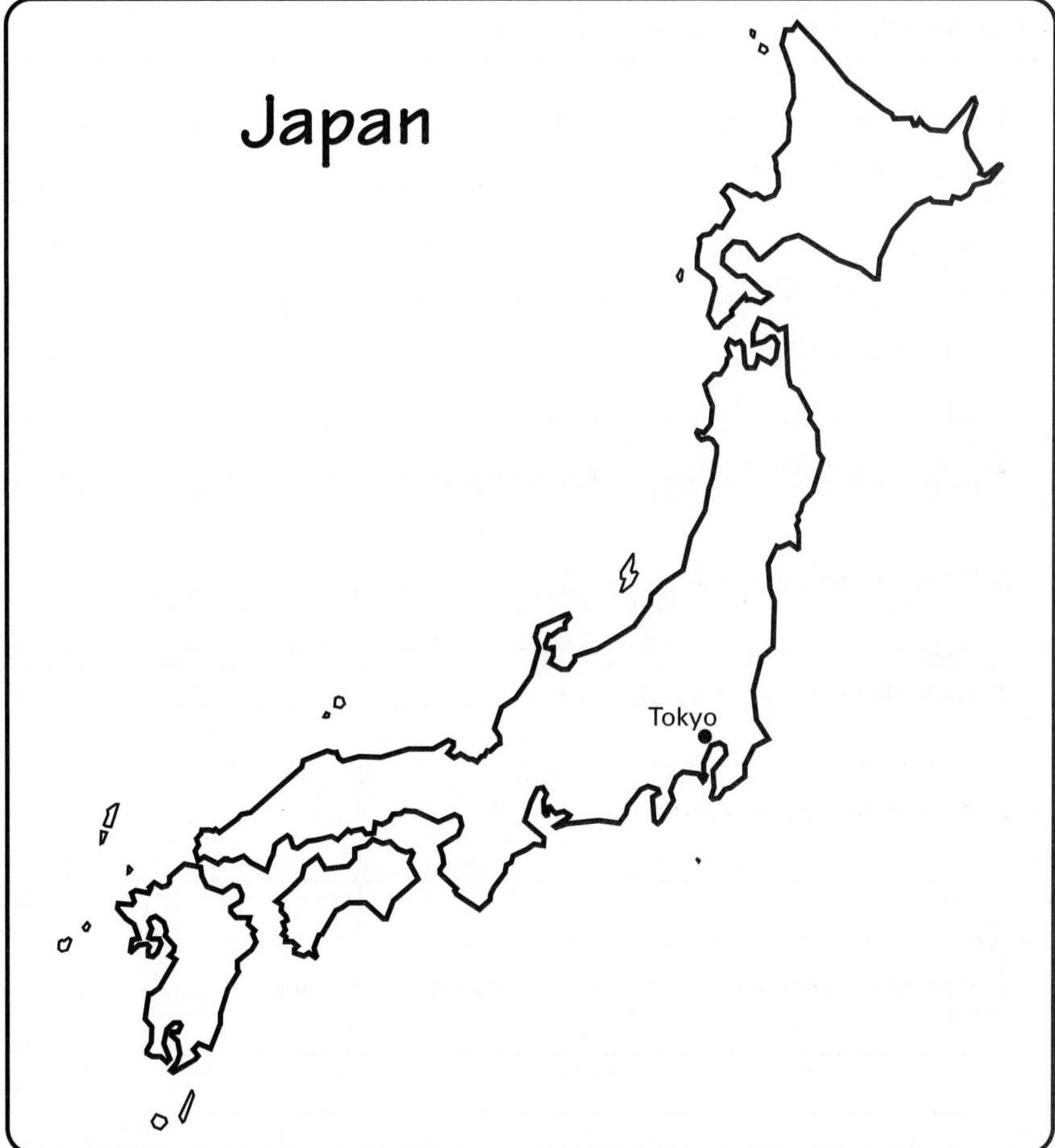

Developing Respect and Empathy

I Know What You Mean: Death and Remembrance

Name_____ Date _____

Directions: Refer to encyclopedias and/or other reference books to answer the questions below. If you need more writing space, use the back side of this paper.

1. What type of bomb was dropped on Hiroshima? _____

2. Was this kind of bomb dropped anywhere else?_____

   _____

3. How were the targets selected? _____

   _____

4. When was the bomb dropped? _____

5. Who dropped the bomb? _____

6. What were some of the reasons for dropping this type of bomb? _____

   _____

   _____

   _____

7. What effect did this bomb have on Japan? _____

   _____

   _____

   _____

8. What effect did this bomb have on the rest of the world? _____

   _____

   _____

   _____

Developing Respect and Empathy

I Know How You Feel: Death and Remembrance

Purpose:

to give students the opportunity to experience (within the safety of literature) respect and empathy for someone who is dying or someone who is grieving

Materials:

◆ encyclopedias and other reference books

◆ a large world map and/or globe

◆ *Sadako and the Thousand Cranes* by Eleanor Coerr (Dell, 1979)

◆ copies of page 130, one for each student

◆ copies of page 131, one for each student

◆ writing paper

◆ pens or pencils

Activity—Part 1:

Reread *Sadako and the Thousand Paper Cranes* aloud to your class. Do not forget to reread the prologue and the epilogue also. Have students use references to find out about origami.

Next, ask your students to fold their own paper cranes following the directions on page 130. Send the cranes to the city of Hiroshima in Japan with a letter. In the letter ask that they be added to the cranes placed under Sadako's statue on the next Peace Day.

Activity—Part 2:

Have your students try writing haiku poems about Sadako and her paper cranes. Pass out the activity sheet on page 131 and encourage everyone to try. Share the resulting poems. Be sure to follow the publishing suggestions at the bottom of the activity sheet.

Evaluation and Processing:

Discuss Peace Day . . . Peace Day is on August 6. This year we might all do something to celebrate that day. What could each person do? What would be appropriate? (If you are in year-round school, this would make a good midsummer festival.)

Developing Respect and Empathy

I Know How You Feel: Death and Remembrance

Follow the steps below to make your own paper cranes.

1. Fold an 8'' (20 cm) square paper into eighths and then unfold.

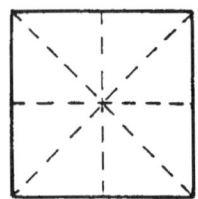

2. Using a diagonal fold as the center, fold the left and right edges into the center line to make a kite shape.

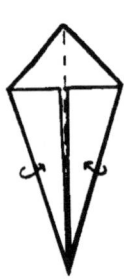

3. Repeat kite fold on each corner. Your opened paper should be creased as shown.

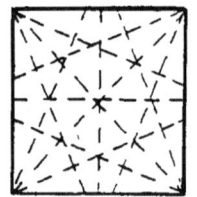

4. Fold the paper in half to make a triangle. Hold it at the star and fold the right side up to meet the top of the triangle.

5. Release the fold and make the same fold inside out, with the fold coming between the front and back of the large triangle. Repeat on left side. Sharpen the crease.

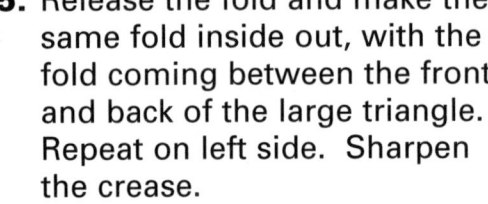

6. Hold the point at the star and fold down the top flap at the broken line. Turn the shape over and repeat the fold on the other side.

  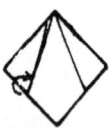  

7. Fold down the right flap at the broken line. Release and make the same fold inside out. Repeat on the left side.

8. Turn the shape as shown and fold the end of the point at the broken line to form the crane's head. Release and make the same fold inside out. Fold down the top flap at the broken line to make a wing. Turn over and fold the other wing.

9. Roll the wings around a pencil to give a curved shape.

Developing Respect and Empathy

I Know How You Feel: Death and Remembrance

Name_____ Date _____

Life is a journey
Up and down the tall mountains
And not around them.

The short poem above is a haiku. A haiku is a type of poem that originated in Japan hundreds of years ago. It is a very short poem consisting of one thought and seems to reflect the beauty and simplicity of Buddhist ideas. A haiku is usually written about nature, but it can express one thought about other subjects, too. It is expressed in 17 syllables written in three lines which do not rhyme. The first and last lines each have five syllables; the middle line has seven.

(5) Life is a journey

(7) Up and down the tall mountains

(5) And not around them.

Check by reading this haiku aloud and clapping the syllables. How many claps for "Life"? (one) For "is"? (one) For "a"? (one) For "journey"? (two) Continue this process for the other two lines.

Find a book of haiku poetry in the school or public library and read some more examples. Then try to write two haiku poems of your own below. Do not forget to check the number of syllables by clapping.

_____

_____

_____

_____

_____

_____

_____

_____

Be sure to publish: When everyone in your class has written at least one haiku, read them aloud to one another. Then illustrate and display them on a poetry bulletin board. When they are taken down, bind the poems into a book for the classroom library.

All Grade Levels

Are We Making Progress? **Age-Appropriate Concerns**

Can We Get Along? **Using Techniques for Conflict Resolution**

Age-Appropriate Concerns

Competition and Cooperation: Working in Groups

Purpose:

to give students the opportunity to experience and evaluate the benefits of group work

Materials:

- ◆ copies of page 136, one for each student
- ◆ copies of page 137, one for each student
- ◆ encyclopedias and other reference materials and/or library access
- ◆ scratch paper
- ◆ pens or pencils
- ◆ page 134 –136 for teacher reference

If you have had a lot of experience with cooperative group work, you can plunge right into these activities. If not, familiarize yourself with some of the basics by reading pages 134–136.

Activity—Part 1:

Divide the class into small groups. Depending on your students' experiences with working in small groups, you may want to spend some time explaining and assigning roles within the groups or you may be able to just let them go to work.

Pass out copies of page 137. Explain that each group will be doing the required research and will then create a song to be presented to the class. Give them an idea of how much time they will have and make sure that each group has access to the reference materials.

Ask each group to present its "Spider Song" to the whole class. Remind your students of good audience manners and reinforce the idea of making only positive remarks. Have your students vote on the best song. (This will set up a competition situation to be addressed in the next activity, "Competition and Cooperation: Between and Within.")

Activity—Part 2:

Let your students stay in their groups for a day and do all of their work together. On the next day, have them do all of their work individually.

Evaluation and Processing:

Take a poll . . . How many students liked to work in groups? How many students liked to work alone? How many students felt comfortable either way?

Age-Appropriate Concerns

Competition and Cooperation: Working in Groups

Components of Cooperative Learning

There are four basic components of cooperative learning. These components make the difference between cooperative learning and traditional group activities. Many of the group activities you have used in the past can be adapted for cooperative learning by adjusting the activities to include the components listed below.

1. **In cooperative learning all group members need to work together to accomplish the task.** No one is finished until the whole group is finished. The task or activity needs to be designed so that members are not each completing their own parts but are working to complete one product together.

2. **Cooperative learning groups should be heterogeneous.** It is helpful to start by organizing groups so that there is a balance of abilities within and among groups. You may also wish to consider other variables when balancing groups.

3. **Cooperative learning activities need to be designed so that each student contributes to the group and individual group members can be assessed on their performances.** This can be accomplished by assigning each member a role that is essential to the completion of the task or activity. When input must be gathered from all members of the group, no one can go along for a free ride.

4. **Cooperative learning teams need to know the social as well as the academic objectives of a lesson.** Students need to know what they are expected to learn and how they are supposed to be working together to accomplish the learning. Students need to process or think and talk about how they worked on social skills. They also need to evaluate how well their group worked on accomplishing the academic objective. Social skills are not something that students automatically know; these skills need to be taught.

Age-Appropriate Concerns

Competition and Cooperation: Working in Groups

The Teacher's Role During Cooperative Lessons

The teacher's role is quite different during cooperative lessons from what it is during a teacher-directed lesson. The teacher has some important decisions to make prior to the lesson, but when the students are working in cooperative groups, the teacher's role is facilitator instead of trainer. When things are running smoothly, the teacher should circulate and observe how the teams are working.

Teachers may need to intervene in the following situations:

- Get the group back on target if they are unsure of what to do.

- Give immediate feedback to the group on how they are progressing with the task or activity.

- Clarify something or give further information to the whole class after observing a general difficulty of mastery.

- Assist in the development of social skills through praise and group reflection.

- Encourage or congratulate the group, depending on how they are progressing with the task.

One caution for teachers is to avoid intervening if the group does not need assistance. Part of collaboration is learning how to discuss what comes next, to examine how the group is doing, and to decide when the group is finished. To successfully progress at this, students need time to work through the different stages and to solve their own problems.

Age-Appropriate Concerns

Competition and Cooperation: Working in Groups

Teachers often find that using job assignments or roles helps students to know what part of the task or activity they are responsible for completing. It gives them specific information on what they need to do to help their team.

Roles that work effectively:

Supplier—gets the materials and supplies for the group

Reporter—reports to the class for the group

Recorder—writes down what the group does, completes the written part of the task or activity, and/or records the group's response during evaluation and processing

Encourager—gives group members praise for their participation and collaboration on the group task or activity

Artist—produces art work

Checker—checks completed work for completeness, neatness, and accuracy

Timekeeper—keeps the group on task and gives time prompts so that the group will complete their task on time

Reader—reads directions, text, or looks up information during group work

Clarifier—summarizes or restates the group's responses, conclusions, or premise

The teacher needs to select roles for group work, depending on the task or activity. Roles need to be taught and modeled for the class. After a period of experience with cooperative learning, specific roles may not be necessary each time for groups that work well together. In this case, groups will naturally divide up the tasks, with group members doing what they like or are especially capable of doing.

Age-Appropriate Concerns

Competition and Cooperation: Working in Groups

Name _____ Group _____

Directions: Do research to answer the following questions.

1. How many legs do spiders have? _____

2. What is the scientific name for spiders? _____

3. Name two poisonous spiders: _____

4. What is the largest spider? _____

5. Do all spiders spin webs? _____

Use all of the information gathered from your research to make up a song about spiders to be sung to the tune of "Yankee Doodle." Rehearse your song until you are ready to perform it for your classmates. All members of your group must participate in the performance of the song.

_____

Yankee Doodle went to town

_____

Riding on a pony;

_____

Stuck a feather in his hat

_____

And called it Macaroni.

_____

Yankee Doodle keep it up.

_____

Yankee Doodle Dandy.

_____

Mind the music and the steps

_____

And with the girls be handy.

Age-Appropriate Concerns

Competition and Cooperation: Between and Within

Purpose:

to give students the opportunity to compare and contrast the ideas of cooperation and competition and decide when each is appropriate

Materials:

- ◆ copies of page 139, one for each student
- ◆ copies of page 140, one for each student
- ◆ dictionaries
- ◆ pens or pencils

Activity—Part 1:

Ask your students to complete page 139. Then tell your students . . . In the last activity you worked in a group to create a silly song. You *cooperated* or worked together. Then you presented your song to the class, and we voted on the best song. That was an example of *competition*; each group tried to be better than the others in order to win.

Cooperation happens within a group. Competition happens among groups.

Can you think of any other examples of cooperation and competition? (within and among classes, teams, schools, political parties, states, countries, etc.)

What effect does the competition among groups have on the amount of cooperation within those groups? Discuss. (For example, do teams work together better when they know a big game with another team is coming up? Do people in a country pull together and cooperate because of the threat of war?)

Activity—Part 2:

Pass out the writing prompt (page 140) and give your students ample time to think and write. If you use the writing process, this can be a "quick write" or a first draft. Then give the students the opportunity to later do the editing and revising steps.

When the papers are completed (for your purposes), ask for volunteers to read their pieces aloud to the group. Remind the audience of good listening manners and the necessity for making positive comments.

Evaluation and Processing:

Discuss the activity . . . Now we know now what the differences are between cooperation and competition, but what did you discover about the relationship between these two ways of acting? What do you know now that you did not know before? Do you have any new ideas about how to motivate people to be cooperative?

Age-Appropriate Concerns

Competition and Cooperation: Between and Within

Name _____ Date _____

Directions: Use a dictionary, as needed, to complete the statements below.

Competition means _____

_____

_____

_____

_____

Cooperation means _____

_____

_____

_____

_____

The main difference between competition and cooperation is _____

_____

_____

_____

_____

Age-Appropriate Concerns

Competition and Cooperation: Between and Within

Name_____ Date _____

Writing Situation:

We have been talking about cooperation and competition and the relationship between these two ways of acting. Based on what we have learned and discussed, can you think of a situation that would motivate the countries of the world to stop competing and start cooperating with one another?

Directions for Writing:

Think of a plan for motivating the countries of the world to cooperate with one another. Describe your idea in enough detail and back it up with enough reasons so that your reader (or listener) will be convinced that it would work. Express your thoughts in complete sentences, and use additional sheets of paper if you need to.

_____

_____

_____

_____

_____

_____

_____

_____

_____

_____

_____

_____

_____

Age-Appropriate Concerns

Competition and Cooperation: Interpersonal or Intrapersonal

Purpose:

to give students the opportunity to think about their own intelligences and decide which learning style would be most likely to be cooperative or competitive

Materials:

- ◆ copies of page 142, one for each student
- ◆ copies of page 143, one for each student
- ◆ copies of page 144, one for each student
- ◆ pens or pencils

Activity—Part 1:

Pass out copies of pages 142 and 143. Depending on the age and experience of your students, read and discuss the definitions on these two activity sheets with them or let them do the work on their own.

When the activity sheets have been completed, get your students' opinions about which type of intelligence would probably be most cooperative and which would be most competitive. Discuss. (Be sure to tell them that it is possible for one person to have both of these intelligences and to be able to switch back and forth.)

Activity—Part 2:

After your discussion of these two types of intelligences, pass out copies of page 144 and ask your students to analyze themselves, using the definitions on the two activity sheets. Meet as a large group to share and discuss the results.

Evaluation and Processing:

Discuss the activity . . . Have you ever wondered why you work well with people? Have you ever wondered why you do not like group work and prefer to work by yourself? Have you ever wondered why you do not mind switching back and forth from one method to the other? Did you know that these preferences are shared by many people? Do you think that it is possible to learn to have another intelligence? How would you go about it? Would it be worth trying? Would you like to be more cooperative or more competitive, or are you happy with this aspect of yourself the way you are now?

Age-Appropriate Concerns

Competition and Cooperation: Interpersonal or Intrapersonal

Name_____ Date _____

Definition

Interpersonal Intelligence: It means tending to turn outward and connect with other people as part of the thinking process. It is expressed in the enjoyment of friends and social activities of all kinds and in not liking to be alone. People with this kind of intelligence enjoy working in groups, learn while interacting and cooperating, and often serve as peacemakers in case of disagreements, both in school and at home. They are the people who love cooperative learning groups, student council meetings, and running for office.

What picture or symbol could you use to remind yourself of what is meant by interpersonal intelligence? Make a sketch of your idea in the space below.

Age-Appropriate Concerns

Competition and Cooperation: Interpersonal or Intrapersonal

Name_____ Date _____

Definition

Intrapersonal Intelligence: It means tending to turn inward to explore one's own thoughts and feelings as part of the thinking process. It is shown through a deep awareness of inner feelings. This is the intelligence that allows people to understand themselves, their abilities, and their options. People with intrapersonal intelligence tend to be independent and self-directed and have strong opinions on controversial subjects. (Controversial subjects are subjects about which people disagree.) They have a great sense of self-confidence and enjoy working on their own projects and just being alone.

What picture or symbol could you use to remind yourself of what is meant by intrapersonal intelligence? Make a sketch of your idea in the space below.

Age-Appropriate Concerns

Competition and Cooperation: Interpersonal or Intrapersonal

Name_____ Date _____

Directions: Finish the statement which most pertains to you. Include examples about yourself which support the statement.

I think my intelligence style is mainly interpersonal because_____

_____

_____

_____

_____

I think my intelligence style is mainly intrapersonal because_____

_____

_____

_____

I think my intelligence style is interpersonal and intrapersonal because_____

_____

_____

_____

Age-Appropriate Concerns

Rules and Self-Direction: Famous People

Purpose:

to give students the opportunity to think about whether they prefer to follow rules that have been made for them or to exercise self-direction

Materials:

- ◆ copies of page 146, one for each student
- ◆ copies of page 147, one for each student
- ◆ encyclopedias and other reference books and/or library access
- ◆ pens or pencils

Activity—Part 1:

Discuss with the class some famous people from your social studies text. Ask your students if they think those famous people followed the rules or if they were self-directed. (Opinions will differ on this.) Also ask when it is important to follow the rules and when it is important to be more self-directed.

Pass out copies of page 146 and have your students choose three people to research, using the reference books in your classroom or the school library. They should decide whether the three people were self-directed or followed the rules. They will need to give examples to justify their opinions.

Meet as a large group to share and discuss the information and opinions.

Activity—Part 2:

Have each student use the directions on page 147 to complete the writing activity. Encourage them to justify the opinions they assert on this subject. When your students have finished writing, ask them to share what they wrote with the rest of the class. Discuss.

Evaluation and Processing:

Make sure that your students give reasons to back up opinions in these exercises. Ask them . . . Why do you think that? What makes you think so? Are you generalizing from the information you found in the research you did?

Age-Appropriate Concerns

Rules and Self-Direction: Famous People

Name_____ Date _____

Directions: Choose three famous people from history. Do enough research on each person to decide if you feel he or she followed the rules or was self-directed (circle one). Give an example to support each of your opinions.

1. _____ was self-directed.
   followed the rules.

   For example: _____

   _____

   _____

   _____

2. _____ was self-directed.
   followed the rules.

   For example: _____

   _____

   _____

   _____

3. _____ was self-directed.
   followed the rules.

   For example: _____

   _____

   _____

   _____

Age-Appropriate Concerns

Rules and Self-Direction: *Famous People*

Name_____ Date _____

Directions: You have been considering whether some of the famous people in history followed the rules or were self-directed. Make a generalization on this subject about the people you studied. In general, do you think most of the historical figures followed the rules, or were they self-directed? Decide what you think and write one or two paragraphs in which you tell why. Use the back of this paper if you need more space.

I think most famous people _____because

_____

_____

_____

_____

_____

_____

_____

_____

_____

_____

_____

_____

_____

_____

Age-Appropriate Concerns

Rules and Self-Directions: Plan Your Career

Purpose:

to give students the opportunity to think about whether they prefer to follow rules that have been made for them or to exercise self-direction and to apply this information to career planning

Materials:

- ◆ copies of page 149, one for each student
- ◆ copies of page 150, one for each student
- ◆ pens or pencils

Activity—Part 1:

Discuss a variety of careers. Which ones require people to follow a set of strict rules? Which ones reward people who are self-directed?

Pass out copies of page 149 and have your students meet in groups to brainstorm careers that fit into the two categories: "Rules" and "Self-Direction."

Meet as a large group to share and discuss the information and opinions.

Activity—Part 2:

Ask the students to think about themselves and how they feel about rules and self-direction. Are there some careers that they should think about? Some careers that they should avoid? Pass out copies of page 150 and ask your students to write a paragraph or two about their own career options in light of what they have been learning both about careers and about their own feelings. When they have finished writing, ask for volunteers to share what they wrote with the rest of the class. Discuss.

Evaluation and Processing:

Discuss the activity . . . Have any of our discussions made you take a second look at possible career choices? If a self-directed person has a great desire to follow a career with many rules, would he or she be able to adjust? Could a person who is comfortable with rules be happy in a career that requires self-direction?

Age-Appropriate Concerns

Rules and Self-Direction: Plan Your Career

Name_____ Date _____

Directions: Some careers require people to follow strict guidelines (Rules). Other careers allow people to guide themselves (Self-Direction). Both options have their pros and cons, and some people naturally work better in one situation or the other. List as many careers as you can for these two categories.

Rules	Self-Direction

Age-Appropriate Concerns

Rules and Self-Direction: Plan Your Career

Name_____ Date _____

Directions: You have been considering careers in which it is necessary to follow the rules and careers that require self-direction. Write a couple of paragraphs telling what you should think about before you decide on a career.

Before I decide on a career I should think about _____

_____

_____

_____

_____

_____

_____

_____

_____

_____

_____

_____

_____

_____

_____

_____

_____

Age-Appropriate Concerns

Equal Treatment and Special Circumstances: Fair or Not Fair

Purpose:

to give students the opportunity to compare the ideal of equal treatment with the reality of special circumstances

Materials:

- ◆ copies of page 152, one for each student
- ◆ copies of page 153, one for each student
- ◆ dictionaries
- ◆ pens or pencils

Activity—Part 1:

Have the students complete page 152 to familiarize themselves with the words and concepts of this lesson. When they have finished the activity sheet, meet as a large group to compare and discuss their definitions.

Activity—Part 2:

Students in grades five through eight like everything to be fair. But, as we all must learn, life is not always fair. Discuss the situations described below. Then ask your students to think of other circumstances that might require special, rather than equal, treatment.

- ◆ There will be a physical fitness test today that you must pass. But your right leg is broken and will be in a cast until next month. Do you think you should get special treatment?

- ◆ You dropped your glasses on the bus this morning and someone stepped on them. Should you get a bad grade because you cannot read words and numbers?

- ◆ In order for the game to be really fair, the same rules should apply to everyone. But Zack is in a wheelchair and cannot run. Will you still let him play?

Pass out copies of page 153 and ask the students to complete it. When all the students have finished this assignment, ask for volunteers to read their pieces aloud to the rest of the class. Discuss.

Evaluation and Processing:

This can be a delicate topic if there are students in your class who are sensitive about having some special circumstances of their own. You may want to skip this, only do part of it, or use the opportunity to shed some light on a dark area.

Age-Appropriate Concerns

Equal Treatment and Special Circumstances: Fair or Not Fair

Name_____ Date _____

Directions: Use a dictionary to help you define these terms.

Equal means_____

_____

_____

Treatment means_____

_____

_____

Equal treatment means _____

_____

_____

Special means_____

_____

_____

Circumstances means_____

_____

_____

Special circumstances means _____

_____

Age-Appropriate Concerns

Equal Treatment and Special Circumstances: Fair or Not Fair

Name_____ Date _____

Directions: There are times when equal treatment would not be fair to the people involved. Tell about a time when special circumstances would require special treatment. Make up a situation or describe something from your own experience. Use the back of this paper if you need more writing space.

_____

_____

_____

_____

_____

_____

_____

_____

_____

_____

_____

_____

_____

_____

Age-Appropriate Concerns

Justice and Compassion: A Current Event

Purpose:

to acquaint students with situations in which people have decided or must decide on the relative importance (significance, value, worth, etc.) of justice and compassion

Materials:

◆ copies of page 155, one for each student

◆ copies of page 156, one for each student

◆ dictionaries

◆ pens or pencils

Activity—Part 1:

Pass out copies of page 155 and have your students complete this activity sheet individually or in groups. When the students finish this assignment, meet as a large group to compare and discuss their answers.

Activity—Part 2:

When you feel comfortable about the level of understanding your students have achieved regarding the ideas of justice and compassion, pass out copies of page 156. It can be used as a homework assignment over any period of time that works well for you.

The students can check newspapers on a daily basis until they each find an article that is relevant to the justice versus compassion theme. (You might want to make a daily newspaper available in the classroom for the students who do not have access to a newspaper at home.) Reports can be made and discussed as the students return their assignments.

After each current event has been discussed, post it on a bulletin board.

Note: Explain the meaning of the term "dateline" as it refers to an item in the newspaper.

Evaluation and Processing:

Discuss the activity . . . Are justice and compassion common concerns? Our system of laws and courts is called the "justice system." Why do we not have a "compassion system"?

Age-Appropriate Concerns

Justice and Compassion: A Current Event

Name _____ Date _____

Directions: Use a dictionary, as needed, to complete this activity sheet.

Justice means _____

_____

_____

_____

Compassion means _____

_____

_____

_____

The main difference between justice and compassion is _____

_____

_____

_____

Is it always necessary or wise to be compassionate? _____

_____

_____

_____

Age-Appropriate Concerns

Justice and Compassion: A Current Event

Name_____ Date _____

Directions: Look for a newspaper article about a current event which shows some sort of conflict between justice and compassion. Read the article, describe the conflict, and reflect upon your opinions of the subject below. If possible, attach the newspaper clipping.

Newspaper: _____

Dateline: _____

Topic: _____

In summary, the conflict between justice and compassion in this article is _____

_____

_____

_____

_____

_____

_____

_____

_____

_____

_____

_____

_____

_____

Using Techniques for Conflict Resolution

Assertiveness: I Can Stand Up for Myself

Purpose:

to encourage students to use assertive rather than passive or aggressive behaviors

Materials:

- ◆ copies of page 158, one for each student
- ◆ copies of pages 159 and 160, one set for each student
- ◆ dictionaries
- ◆ pens or pencils

Activity—Part 1:

Tell the students . . . We are going to learn about three types of behaviors—passive, aggressive, and assertive. Very briefly, a *passive* person gives in, an *aggressive* person gets angry, and an *assertive* person stands up for himself or herself.

Many adults go to classes to learn how to be assertive. Some of these adults have found that they are not able to say "no" to requests from other people. Others always react with anger to situations that could be handled assertively instead of aggressively. When you are assertive, you do not give in and you do not get angry. You are in a good position to negotiate and compromise (which are ways of reaching agreements that we will be learning more about).

Here is a situation with examples of the three types of responses:

A friend of yours is in charge of a committee that collects papers and cans to be recycled. He wants you to join the committee which meets every Saturday morning from 8:00 a.m. until noon. You already have softball practice on Saturdays from 1:00 p.m. until 4:00 p.m. and your mother expects you to do some chores for her too. You really do not want to be on the recycling committee, but your friend is putting a lot of pressure on you, and you know his feelings will be hurt if you refuse.

Passive response: Sure. I'll be there, but I have to leave in time for practice.

Aggressive response: Stop bugging me! I don't want to be on your stupid committee!

Assertive response: I'm sorry, but I can't be there. My Saturdays are already full.

Things to notice:

- ◆ An assertive statement is polite, but it is also honest.
- ◆ An assertive statement shows self-respect as well as respect for the other person.

Activity—Part 2:

Divide your students into small groups to define the terms on page 158. Then, pass out the situation activity sheets (pages 159 and 160) to the students to discuss and complete. When all of the groups have finished their activity sheets, meet again as a large group to compare and discuss the results.

Evaluation and Processing:

Discuss the activity . . . Did you recognize yourself in any of these situations? Are you usually passive, aggressive, or assertive?

Using Techniques for Conflict Resolution

Assertiveness: I Can Stand Up for Myself

Student _____ Group _____

Directions: Work with your group to define the following terms. You may use dictionaries and/or other reference books.

Passive means _____

_____

_____

_____

_____

Aggressive means_____

_____

_____

_____

_____

Assertive means _____

_____

_____

_____

_____

Using Techniques for Conflict Resolution

Assertiveness: I Can Stand Up for Myself

Student _____ Group _____

Directions: Work with your group to write responses for the following situations.

Remember . . .

1. An assertive statement is polite, but it is also honest.
2. An assertive statement shows self-respect as well as respect for the other person.

> **Situation One:**
> Someone you thought was one of your best friends is planning a big overnight party. Everybody is talking about it, and so far you are the only one who has not received an invitation. Your feelings are hurt, and you are also feeling embarrassed about being left out.

Passive response:_____

_____

_____

_____

Aggressive response:_____

_____

_____

_____

Assertive response:_____

_____

_____

_____

Using Techniques for Conflict Resolution

Assertiveness: I Can Stand Up for Myself

Student _____ Group _____

Directions: Work with your group to write responses for the following situations.

Remember . . .

1. An assertive statement is polite, but it is also honest.
2. An assertive statement shows self-respect, as well as respect for the other person.

Situation Two:

A teacher wants you to lead a classroom committee that will meet during lunch recess every day for a month. He asked you to do this because you are a good student and your classroom behavior is excellent. You know that the only reason you are able to study hard and maintain your good behavior is because you can look forward to blowing off steam at lunch recess by playing with your friends.

Passive response:_____

_____

_____

_____

Aggressive response:_____

_____

_____

_____

Assertive response:_____

_____

_____

Using Techniques for Conflict Resolution

Assertiveness: I Can Say No

Purpose:

to give students information about different ways to say no

Materials:

- ◆ copies of pages 162–164, one set for each student
- ◆ pens or pencils

Activity—Part 1:

Tell the students . . . There are sometimes when being safe is much more important than being either honest or polite and when keeping your self-respect is more important than showing respect for the other person. These are situations in which you are being asked to do things that are dangerous or against the law. In these cases, although you could be passive or aggressive, your assertiveness will need to be more unequivocal: that is, you should make it clear that there are no other choices.

There are several ways to handle extreme situations:

You can make a clear *"I"* statement. (Say what you think and feel.)

You can put the responsibility somewhere else. (Blame your parents.)

You can use the "broken record" technique. (Say the same thing over and over.)

Walk (or run) away. (Leave the situation.)

Report it. (Get away any way you can and tell an adult.)

Here is a situation. Which responses would work here? (Discuss choices.)

A friend of yours has agreed to fight someone after school in the park. He wants you to come with him. The person he is going to fight belongs to a gang. On top of that, your school has rules about fights that include suspension for anyone who is even watching. You are worried for him, but you are even more worried for yourself.

Clear statement: I think it's a bad idea. I am not going to be there.

Responsibility: My mother would ground me forever if I got suspended!

Broken record: No, no, no, no, no!

Walk away: (Just go home after school.)

Report: (Tell someone in authority what is going to happen.)

Activity—Part 2:

Divide your students into small groups to discuss and work on the activity sheets (pages 162–164). Then, come back together as a large group to compare and discuss the results.

Evaluation and Processing:

Discuss the activity . . . Which situation would be the most difficult to be in? Have you ever had to deal with situations like these in real life? What did you do? If you had to deal with situations like these now, would you do anything differently?

Using Techniques for Conflict Resolution

Assertiveness: I Can Say No

Student _____ Group _____

Directions: Work with your group to choose at least two responses for the following situation. Write the dialogue that you imagine would take place. Remember, in a dangerous situation, safety is more important than being polite or honest.

Situation One:

The person you usually walk to school with is one of the most popular girls in school. She has been showing you all of her new makeup and jewelry. This morning she invited you to walk home with her and to join her on a shoplifting expedition. You are afraid she will tell everyone if you refuse.

First response: _____

_____

_____

_____

_____

Second response: _____

_____

_____

_____

_____

Using Techniques for Conflict Resolution

Assertiveness: I Can Say No

Student _____ Group _____

Directions: Work with your group to choose at least two responses for the following situation. Write the dialogue that you imagine would take place. Remember, in a dangerous situation, safety is more important than being polite or honest.

Situation Two:
You have a friend who has been neglecting his school assignments, using new slang, missing soccer practices, and generally acting differently than he used to act. One afternoon, he asks you to try some "substance" he is using. If you do, he will be able to get more for both of you.

First response:_____

_____

_____

_____

_____

_____

Second response:_____

_____

_____

_____

_____

_____

_____

Using Techniques for Conflict Resolution

Assertiveness: I Can Say No

Directions: Work with your group to choose at least two responses for the following situation. Write the dialogue that you imagine would take place. Remember, in a dangerous situation, safety is more important than being polite or honest.

Situation Three:

When you are on your way to the library, a car pulls up beside you and a man (whom you do not recognize) leans out. He says that your mother has been in an accident and was taken to the hospital. He offers to take you there.

First response: _____

_____

_____

_____

_____

Second response: _____

_____

_____

_____

_____

Using Techniques for Conflict Resolution

Negotiation: I Can Think of a Plan

Purpose:

to give students information about how to use negotiation to resolve conflicts

Materials:

- ◆ copies of pages 166–170, one set for each student
- ◆ pens or pencils

Activity—Part 1:

Tell the students today we are going to learn about negotiation. Negotiation is a bargaining process that helps people on opposite sides of an issue to reach an agreement. The first step in negotiation is for each side to state its demands or tell what it wants. Each side has a plan.

In real life these plans usually contain extra things that the people do not really care about. They are then prepared to give up these things in exchange for things that the other side will give up. (This prepares them for the next step which is compromise.)

The following is a situation with examples of plans offered by two opposite sides.

> Your class is almost evenly divided over the question of extra-credit work. Half of the class wants it to count toward their grades; half of the class does not. Your teacher has suggested that each side of the issue should come up with a plan and negotiate a solution.

Plan of the students against extra credit:

- ◆ Grades should be based on required work so that no extra work is needed for an A grade.
- ◆ Extra-credit work could earn bonus points to be applied toward special privileges.
- ◆ Extra credit could be applied to the grades of students getting D's and F's but only to bring those grades up to C's.

Plan of the students for extra credit:

- ◆ No one should be able to get an A grade without doing some extra-credit work.
- ◆ Students should be able to earn special privileges through a system not based on grades.
- ◆ Extra-credit points should count toward the total grades no matter what the students earned on the basic work.

Discuss these plans. Will these opposing sides have any space to work toward a compromise?

Activity—Part 2:

Divide the class into groups and pass out the activity sheets (pages 166–170). Tell the students to make up plans for the situations. Then, meet as a large group to compare and discuss the results. (Note: To save paper or to shorten this activity, you may want to give each group a different situation instead of giving all of the situations to all of the groups. To do this you will need exactly five groups.)

Evaluation and Processing:

Discuss the activity . . . Were you able to allow room for compromise in your plans? Was it hard or easy?

Using Techniques for Conflict Resolution

Negotiation: I Can Think of a Plan

Student _____ Group _____

Directions: Work with your group to write a plan for each side of the following situation.

> **Situation One:** Your school has a working kitchen and the food is really good, especially breakfast. However, in an effort to cut costs, the school district is considering closing the kitchen and either having food brought in from the district's central kitchen or inviting several fast food businesses to take part in a food court.

In favor of keeping the school kitchen: _____

_____

_____

_____

In favor of bringing food in from the central district kitchen: _____

_____

_____

_____

In favor of having a fast food court: _____

_____

_____

_____

Note: Save this completed activity sheet for the next two lessons.

Using Techniques for Conflict Resolution

Negotiation: I Can Think of a Plan

Student _____ Group _____

Directions: Work with your group to write a plan for each side of the following situation.

> **Situation Two:** You want to play in a football league with real uniforms, equipment, and football fields. Your mother wants you to play touch football so that you will not get hurt. Your dad wants you to play golf because it is a sport that you can play for your whole life and also because he is looking forward to having you play with him.

In favor of playing football: _____

_____

_____

_____

In favor of playing touch football: _____

_____

_____

_____

In favor of playing golf: _____

_____

_____

_____

Note: Save this completed activity sheet for the next two lessons.

Using Techniques for Conflict Resolution

Negotiation: I Can Think of a Plan

Student _____   Group _____

Directions: Work with your group to write a plan for each side of the following situation.

Situation Three: Your family is having a difference of opinion about how the kids should get their spending money. The kids want to get allowances every week to be used for entertainment. Your mother feels that the kids should earn money by doing chores. Your dad thinks it would be great if everyone got a paper route.

In favor of weekly allowances: _____

_____

_____

_____

In favor of earning money by doing chores: _____

_____

_____

_____

In favor of getting paper routes: _____

_____

_____

_____

Note: Save this completed activity sheet for the next two lessons.

Using Techniques for Conflict Resolution

Negotiation: I Can Think of a Plan

Student _____ Group _____

Directions: Work with your group to write a plan for each side of the following situation.

> **Situation Four:** Your class is planning a field trip that will cost $5.00 per student. The school district is short on money so the teacher suggests that each student should pay his or her own way. The students who cannot bring $5.00 think that the school district should pay. A few students who are trying to be helpful suggest collecting and redeeming recyclable items to raise the money.

In favor of having the school district pay for the trip: _____

_____

_____

_____

In favor of students paying their own way: _____

_____

_____

_____

In favor of raising the money through recycling efforts: _____

_____

_____

_____

Note: Save this completed activity sheet for the next two lessons.

Using Techniques for Conflict Resolution

Negotiation: I Can Think of a Plan

Student _____ Group _____

Directions: Work with your group to write a plan for each side of the following situation.

> **Situation Five:** Your class will be putting on a play at the winter assembly. Some people want the teacher to assign the parts. Others want to try out for the parts. A third group wants the parts to be awarded on the basis of grades; students who have A's will get the lead parts.

In favor of having the teacher assign the parts: _____

_____

_____

_____

In favor of having the students try out for the parts: _____

_____

_____

_____

In favor of awarding parts on the basis of grades: _____

_____

_____

_____

Note: Save this completed activity sheet for the next two lessons.

Using Techniques for Conflict Resolution

Negotiation: I Can Guess How You Feel

Purpose:

to give students information about how to express strong feelings that may arise during the negotiation process

Materials:

- ◆ completed activity sheets from the previous lesson (pages 166–170)
- ◆ copies of page 172, one for each student
- ◆ pens or pencils

Activity—Part 1:

Tell the students people often have strong feelings about the plans they offer for the purposes of negotiation. While they may not always express these feelings, it helps to be able to acknowledge them and to realize that the people "on the other side of the negotiation table" may have strong feelings too. Remember the plans for and against having extra-credit work. What strong feelings might the people who offered the plans have had?

Plan of the students against extra credit:
- ◆ Grades should be based on required work so that no extra work is needed for an A grade.
- ◆ Extra-credit work could earn bonus points to be applied toward special privileges.
- ◆ Extra credit could be applied to the grades of students getting D's and F's but only to bring those grades up to C's.
  (The people who did not have time to do extra work would probably have the strongest feelings about this plan.)

Plan of the students for extra credit:
- ◆ No one should be able to get an A grade without doing some extra-credit work.
- ◆ Students should be able to earn special privileges through a system not based on grades.
- ◆ Extra-credit points should count toward the total grades no matter what the students earned on the basic work.
  (The people who were doing less than excellent basic work would probably have the strongest feelings about this plan.)

Activity—Part 2:

Divide your students into small groups to consider the plans they made up for the situations in the last lesson. Ask them to pick two situations and tell them to speculate about the feelings of the people who might have taken the various sides in their plans. (The students can detail these opinions on their copies of page 172.)   Meet as a large group to compare and discuss the results.

Evaluation and Processing:

Discuss the activity . . . How did you go about deciding on the feelings? Did you base your ideas on how you would have felt yourself or how someone you know might have felt?

Using Techniques for Conflict Resolution

Negotiation: I Can Guess How You Feel

Student _____ Group _____

Directions: Pick two of the situations from the last lesson. Think about the plans that you wrote for each situation and consider how the people on the various sides might have felt. Who would feel the most strongly about each of the plans? Write about the feelings below.

Situation: _____

Plan #1 _____

_____

Plan #2 _____

_____

Plan #3 _____

_____

Situation: _____

Plan #1 _____

_____

Plan #2 _____

_____

Plan #3 _____

_____

Note: Save this completed activity sheet for the next lesson.

Using Techniques for Conflict Resolution

Compromise: I Can Meet You in the Middle

Purpose:

to give students information about and practice in reaching compromises

Materials:

- ◆ copies of pages 174–178, one set for each student
- ◆ completed activity sheets from pages 166–170
- ◆ pens or pencils

Activity—Part 1:

Tell the students . . . Today we are going to learn about *compromise*. When people compromise, they meet each other halfway. Each side may give a little (of what they care the least about) to get a little (of what they care the most about).

Remember the situation about extra-credit work? I will read it and its plans out loud for you again. Think of ways that these two sides could compromise. How could they meet each other halfway? Here is the situation:

- ◆ Your class is almost evenly divided over the question of extra-credit work. Half of the class wants it to count toward their grades; half the class does not. Your teacher has suggested that each side of the issue should come up with a plan and negotiate a solution.

Plan of the students against extra credit:

- ◆ Grades should be based on required work so that no extra work is needed for an A grade.
- ◆ Extra-credit work could earn bonus points to be applied toward special privileges.
- ◆ Extra-credit could be applied to the grades of students getting D's and F's but only to bring those grades up to C's.

Plan of the students in favor of extra credit:

- ◆ No one should be able to get an A grade without doing some extra-credit work.
- ◆ Students should be able to earn special privileges through a system not based on grades.
- ◆ Extra-credit points should count toward the total grades no matter what the students earned on the basic work.

Can these people reach a compromise based on these plans? Discuss.

Activity—Part 2:

Divide your students into small groups to come up with compromise ideas that might be acceptable to all of the sides. Tell them to use the situations from pages 166–170 and to write their compromises on pages 174–178. (Note: To save paper or to shorten this activity, you may want to have each group find a compromise to a different situation instead of compromises for all of the situations. To do this you will need exactly five groups.)

Evaluation and Processing:

Discuss the activity . . . Can a compromise ever make everybody completely happy? Were you able to think of ways for the sides in these situations to reach compromises? Was it hard or easy?

Using Techniques for Conflict Resolution

Compromise: I Can Meet You in the Middle

Student _____ Group _____

Directions: With your group, look over the plans that you wrote for the following situation. How might these sides reach a compromise? Write your ideas below.

Situation One: Your school has a working kitchen and the food is really good, especially breakfast. However, in an effort to cut costs, the school district is considering closing the kitchen and either having food brought in from the district's central kitchen or inviting several fast food businesses to take part in a food court.

Compromise Agreement

_____

_____

_____

_____

_____

_____

_____

_____

_____

_____

_____

_____

Using Techniques for Conflict Resolution

Compromise: I Can Meet You in the Middle

Student _____ Group _____

Directions: With your group, look over the plans that you wrote for the following situation. How might these sides reach a compromise? Write your ideas below.

Situation Two: You want to play in a football league with real uniforms, equipment, and football fields. Your mother wants you to play touch football so that you will not get hurt. Your dad wants you to play golf because it is a sport that you can play for your whole life and also because he is looking forward to having you play with him.

Compromise Agreement

_____

_____

_____

_____

_____

_____

_____

_____

_____

_____

_____

_____

_____

Using Techniques for Conflict Resolution

Compromise: I Can Meet You in the Middle

Student _____ Group _____

Directions: With your group, look over the plans that you wrote for the following situation. How might these sides reach a compromise? Write your ideas below.

Situation Three: Your family is having a difference of opinion about how the kids should get their spending money. The kids want to get allowances every week to be used for entertainment. Your mother feels that the kids should earn money by doing chores. Your dad thinks it would be great if everyone got a paper route.

Compromise Agreement

_____

_____

_____

_____

_____

_____

_____

_____

_____

_____

_____

_____

Using Techniques for Conflict Resolution

Compromise: *I Can Meet You in the Middle*

Student _____   Group _____

Directions: With your group, look over the plans that you wrote for the following situation. How might these sides reach a compromise? Write your ideas below.

Situation Four: Your class is planning a field trip that will cost $5.00 per student. The school district is short on money so the teacher suggests that each student should pay his or her own way. The students who cannot bring $5.00 think that the school district should pay. A few students who are trying to be helpful suggest collecting and redeeming recyclable items to raise the money.

Compromise Agreement

_____

_____

_____

_____

_____

_____

_____

_____

_____

_____

_____

Using Techniques for Conflict Resolution

Compromise: I Can Meet You in the Middle

Student _____ Group _____

Directions: With your group, look over the plans that you wrote for the following situation. How might these sides reach a compromise? Write your ideas below.

Situation Five: Your class will be putting on a play at the winter assembly. Some people want the teacher to assign the parts. Others want to try out for the parts. A third group wants the parts to be awarded on the basis of grades; students who have A's will get the lead parts.

Compromise Agreement

_____

_____

_____

_____

_____

_____

_____

_____

_____

_____

_____

_____

_____

_____

Using Techniques for Conflict Resolution

Compromise: I Can Live with This

Purpose:

to give students information about and practice in reaching compromises in everyday school life

Materials:

◆ copies of pages 180 and 181, one set for each student
◆ pens or pencils

Activity—Part 1:

Tell the students . . . Today we are going to learn more about compromising. As we have already learned, when people compromise, they meet each other halfway. Each side may need to give a little to get a little.

We have been looking at situations that might have been important to a number of people. However, compromises take place in everyday circumstances as well as in major situations. When someone expresses a feeling with an *"I"* message and someone else uses active listening to receive the message, there is an opportunity for compromise in the response.

If you use all of the communication formulas we have been discussing, you will finally reach a place where compromise can take place:

First Person: I can't stand it when you bump into me in line! I want you to quit it. (*"I" message*)

Second Person: I understand that you get mad when I bump into you and you want me to quit. (*active listening restated to show comprehension*) But look at it from my side. I can't tell when you are going to stop suddenly. I wish you would signal or something. (*other perspective/"I" message*)

First Person: Okay. I'll try not to stop suddenly. (*compromise response*)

Second Person: And I'll look where I'm going. (*compromise response*)

Ask your students to try acting out the following first person *"I"* statements all the way through the compromise stage.

◆ I feel squished when your chair is so close to mine. I want you to move over.
◆ I'm afraid the teacher will catch you with your headphones on. I wish you would turn off your radio.
◆ I'm sorry you forgot your lunch. I wish you would let me lend you some money.

Activity—Part 2:

Pass out copies of pages 180 and 181 and have your students complete the activity sheets. Meet as a large group to share and compare the results.

Evaluation and Processing:

Discuss the activity . . . Does compromising come more easily to you now? Does it work when no one is watching or checking? When have you tried it?

Using Techniques for Conflict Resolution

Compromise: I Can live with This

Name_____ Date_____

Directions: Read the first person's *"I"* message. Follow the communication steps all the way through to a compromise.

◆ **First Person** (*"I" message*):

I feel furious when you tease me. I wish you would not do that.

◆ **Second Person** (*active listening restated to show comprehension*):

_____

_____

_____

◆ **Second Person** (*other perspective/"I" message*):

_____

_____

_____

◆ **First Person** (*compromise response*):

_____

_____

_____

◆ **Second Person** (*compromise response*):

_____

_____

_____

Using Techniques for Conflict Resolution

Compromise: I Can Live With This

Name_____ Date _____

Directions: Read the first person's "I" message. Follow the communication steps all the way through to a compromise.

◆ **First Person** (*"I" message*):

I feel angry because you don't do your job in the group. I want you to do your share.

◆ **Second Person** (*active listening restated to show comprehension*):

_____

_____

_____

◆ **Second Person** (*other perspective/"I" message*):

_____

_____

_____

◆ **First Person** (*compromise response*):

_____

_____

_____

◆ **Second Person** (*compromise response*):

_____

_____

_____

Using Techniques for Conflict Resolution

Mediation: I Can Help Others

Purpose:

to introduce students to the idea of peer mediation and provide practice in mediating

Materials:

- ◆ copies of page 185, one for each student
- ◆ copies of page 186, one badge for each student
- ◆ copies of page 187, one for each student
- ◆ safety pins
- ◆ laminating materials
- ◆ pens or pencils

Note:

In our efforts to teach students not to be tattletales, we very often make them feel it is wrong to ask for help from an adult. This is just as true in grades five through eight as it is in the lower grades. Although you will probably want your students to learn to be peer mediators, they must still feel assured that the teacher is available to assist in solving problems. If the students have learned to use *"I"* messages, listen actively, speak assertively, offer plans for solutions, and compromise, there will not be as much need for mediation but there will certainly still be some.

Students of all ages need to be protected from bullies. The bully needs to be helped too. More and more research being done in this area shows that bullying is a very serious problem that, left untreated, can result in serious consequences later in school and in adult life.

Bullies and their victims can be identified early on by their behaviors and personality characteristics. An excellent and concise overview of both personality types can be found in *Teaching Students to Get Along* by Lee Canter and Katia Petersen (Lee Canter & Associates, 1995). Both personality types can be helped by activities that build self-esteem.

Activity—Part 1:

Tell the students that they can always ask you for help but that they are now going to learn how to help each other. Students in many schools are forming groups with names such as Peacemakers, Peace Patrol, SAVE (Students Against Violence Everywhere), and so on. Your plan will begin in your own classroom, but if it is successful and helpful to students, they may want to present it to the school and teach others how to use it. Tell them that they may help any classmate who wants help and that you will make a script available for them to use. Remind them that you will always be available for back-up.

Prepare by reviewing some of the earlier lessons about sending information with *"I"* messages, receiving information with active listening, and responding to information with the appropriate behavior. Run through a variety of situations, letting your students practice being peer mediators. Use the formula on page 183.

Using Techniques for Conflict Resolution

Mediation: I Can Help Others (cont.)

Situation: A visibly upset student (let's call her Dina) comes into the classroom after lunch.

Peer Mediator: Do you need help, Dina?

Dina: Frank makes me sick!

Peer Mediator: Can you tell me what is wrong by using an *"I"* message?

Dina: I feel angry and disgusted when Frank calls me names. I want him to stop.

Peer Mediator: Frank, please come and talk to us. Did you hear Dina?

Frank: Yeah.

Peer Mediator: Please use active listening to tell us what Dina said.

Frank: Dina said she feels angry and disgusted when I call her names, and she wants me to stop.

Peer Mediator: Now tell us that in your own words.

Frank: Dina wants me to stop calling her names because it really makes her mad.

Peer Mediator: Is that right, Dina?

Dina: Yes.

Peer Mediator: Can you say anything to make Dina feel better, Frank?

Frank: Sorry, Dina.

Peer Mediator: Is there anything that you can do to make Dina feel better?

Frank: I can stop calling her names.

Peer Mediator: Do you feel okay about that, Dina?

Dina: Yes. Thank you.

Peer Mediator: That was good communication!

Using Techniques for Conflict Resolution

Mediation: I Can Help Others *(cont.)*

Activity—Part 2:

Becoming part of a peer mediation team is a great self-esteem booster for students. You can extend this program to all of your students or have special rules and qualifications for the job. There is something to be said for both approaches. Meeting special requirements is an extra boost for kids; they can be looked up to by others. However, helping others even if you are not perfect yourself can give you added incentive to try. This is entirely up to you, and your decision will probably depend on the makeup of your current group of students and your educational philosophy.

Still another approach is to have the responsibility for being a peer mediator rotate around the classroom, say six students a week. They can wear the badges on page 186 and take a pledge at the beginning of their week.

Peer Mediator Pledge

I promise to be ready and willing to help anyone who asks for help.

I will be polite and respectful to the people whom I help.

I will follow the Peer Mediation Script.

I will ask the teacher for help, if necessary.

Evaluation and Processing:

Discuss your peer mediator program. Ask your students . . . Is this helpful? Are the mediators polite and respectful? Is the script useful? Can you suggest any changes we need to make?

Are you happy with the way the mediators are selected? Have you been a peer mediator? If not, would you like to be one? Why?

Using Techniques for Conflict Resolution

Mediation: I Can Help Others—Script

Mediator Directions: In the case of a conflict, use this script to guide a conversation between the two opposing parties. The blank lines are for the students' names and their responses. You may want to highlight your lines ahead of time for easy referencing.

Peer Mediator: Do you need help,_____?

    First Person's Response:_____

_____

Peer Mediator: Can you tell me what is wrong by using an *"I"* message?

    First Person's Response:_____

_____

*Peer Mediator:*_____, please come and talk to us. Did you hear

_____?

    Second Person's Response:_____

_____

Peer Mediator: Please use active listening to tell us what _____said.

    Second Person's Response:_____

_____

Peer Mediator: Now tell us that in your own words.

    Second Person's Response:_____

_____

Peer Mediator: Is that right,_____?

    First Person's Response:_____

_____

Peer Mediator: Can you say anything to make, _____feel better?

    Second Person's Response:_____

_____

Peer Mediator: Is there anything that you can do to make _____feel better?

    Second Person's Response:_____

_____

Peer Mediator: Do you feel okay about that, _____?

    First Person's Response:_____

_____

Peer Mediator: That was good communication!

Using Techniques for Conflict Resolution

Mediation: I Can Help Others—Badges

Teacher Directions: Write a different student's name on each badge. Cut out and laminate the badges. Use safety pins to attach the badges to clothing.

Using Techniques for Conflict Resolution

Mediation: I Can Help Others—Pledge

Peer Mediator Pledge

I promise to be ready and willing to help anyone who asks for help.

I will be polite and respectful to the people whom I help.

I will follow the Peer Mediation Script.

I will ask the teacher for help, if necessary.

Using Techniques for Conflict Resolution

Mediation: I Can Ask for Help

Purpose:

to provide support for students who need the help of adults in dealing with conflict situations

Materials:

◆ many copies of page 189

Activity—Part 1:

Remind your students that they are supposed to tell you or another adult when someone is being a bully. Make sure that the students know that reporting a bully is not tattling. It is never tattling to report any situation that involves danger or abuse, whether physical or emotional.

Make a Help Box (like a suggestion box) for your classroom and place a stack of "Mediation Requests" (page 189) next to it. Preserve the security of the box by keeping it on your desk. Discuss situations that warrant the use of a mediation request and let your students know that they can request help for someone else, as well as for themselves.

Be aware that the peer culture of pre-adolescents and adolescents is not conducive to "telling on" people, even when there is real danger or abuse. Be sensitive to the needs of your students and if you promise confidentiality, be sure to keep your word.

Activity—Part 2:

Provide many self-esteem building opportunities in your classroom, such as . . .

◆ classroom jobs that highlight responsibility

◆ creative projects that can be recognized

◆ cross-age tutoring to help younger students

◆ classroom offices with real duties

◆ recognition of effort, as well as grades

Evaluation and Processing:

This activity can be considered successful if you never need to use it, if your students are not afraid to use it, or if its use is effective in resolving conflict.

Using Techniques for Conflict Resolution

Mediation: I Can Ask for Help

Teacher Directions: Make many copies of this page. Cut the requests into slips. Place a pile of slips by the Help Box.

Mediation Request

Person needing help _____

This is an emergency. ☐   Please talk to me privately. ☐

Mediation Request

Person needing help _____

This is an emergency. ☐   Please talk to me privately. ☐

Mediation Request

Person needing help _____

This is an emergency. ☐   Please talk to me privately. ☐

Mediation Request

Person needing help _____

This is an emergency. ☐   Please talk to me privately. ☐

Thematic Teaching

Thematic teaching is an instructional method that centers the entire curriculum around a theme. For the duration of a thematic unit, a classroom's literature, content area lessons, and activities all relate and reinforce the chosen topic. Current research into the way the brain acquires knowledge shows that students learn and retain more by practicing and applying their skills in meaningful contexts. When new knowledge can be linked to prior experience and connections between pieces of information are apparent, comprehension is enhanced. Higher level thinking skills which are needed to analyze, synthesize, and evaluate the knowledge can be invoked. In a thematic classroom both teachers and students will be freed from a day that is broken into unrelated segments of isolated drill and practice on skills for which there is no obvious real-life application.

Thematic teaching is a natural technique for the classroom where all modes of communication are utilized and literature is the focus. Units with activities that extend across the curriculum can be developed from the items found in the literature being used or from the subjects being taught. In traditional classrooms, social studies and science topics, for example, can be developed into thematic units with the addition of appropriate literature and activities from other curriculum areas.

Bulletin boards, decorations, and hands-on apparatus related to the theme set the atmosphere of the classroom. Writing, research, cooperative learning projects, community involvement, and authentic assessment procedures are planned by students and teacher together. All elements are drawn together like the threads of a spider web, ultimately capturing student interest and encouraging success.

On the following pages is a complete thematic unit about peace for the intermediate/challenging level. You may wish to use this unit as an introduction to teaching about conflict resolution or as culmination to the conflict resolution lessons.

A Thematic Unit About Peace

Levels:

Intermediate/Challenging

Literature Selection One:

Peace Begins with You by Katherine Scholes (Sierra Club Books, 1990)

Summary:

Peace Begins with You is a beautifully illustrated book which explains the meaning of peace in a way that can be understood by students. It begins at a personal level and expands through national and international levels to include global issues. It explores ways of resolving conflict, stressing those that are not centered on the winner/loser theme.

Literature Selection Two:

The Big Book for Peace edited by Anne Durell and Marilyn Sachs (Dutton Children's Books, 1990)

Summary:

The Big Book for Peace is an anthology of material about peace especially created for this book by a prestigious group of children's authors in response to concern about the current proliferation of books about war and the machines of war.

Teacher Preparation:

Peace Begins with You and *The Big Book for Peace* address the theme of peace from both an internal and an external point of view and, in the case of the second book, from the particular world view of many different authors.

Collect and display other books written by the authors represented in *The Big Book for Peace*.

Collect and display posters and other materials from organizations that are working toward world peace. See page 199 for suggested names and addresses.

Overview of Activities

Setting the Stage

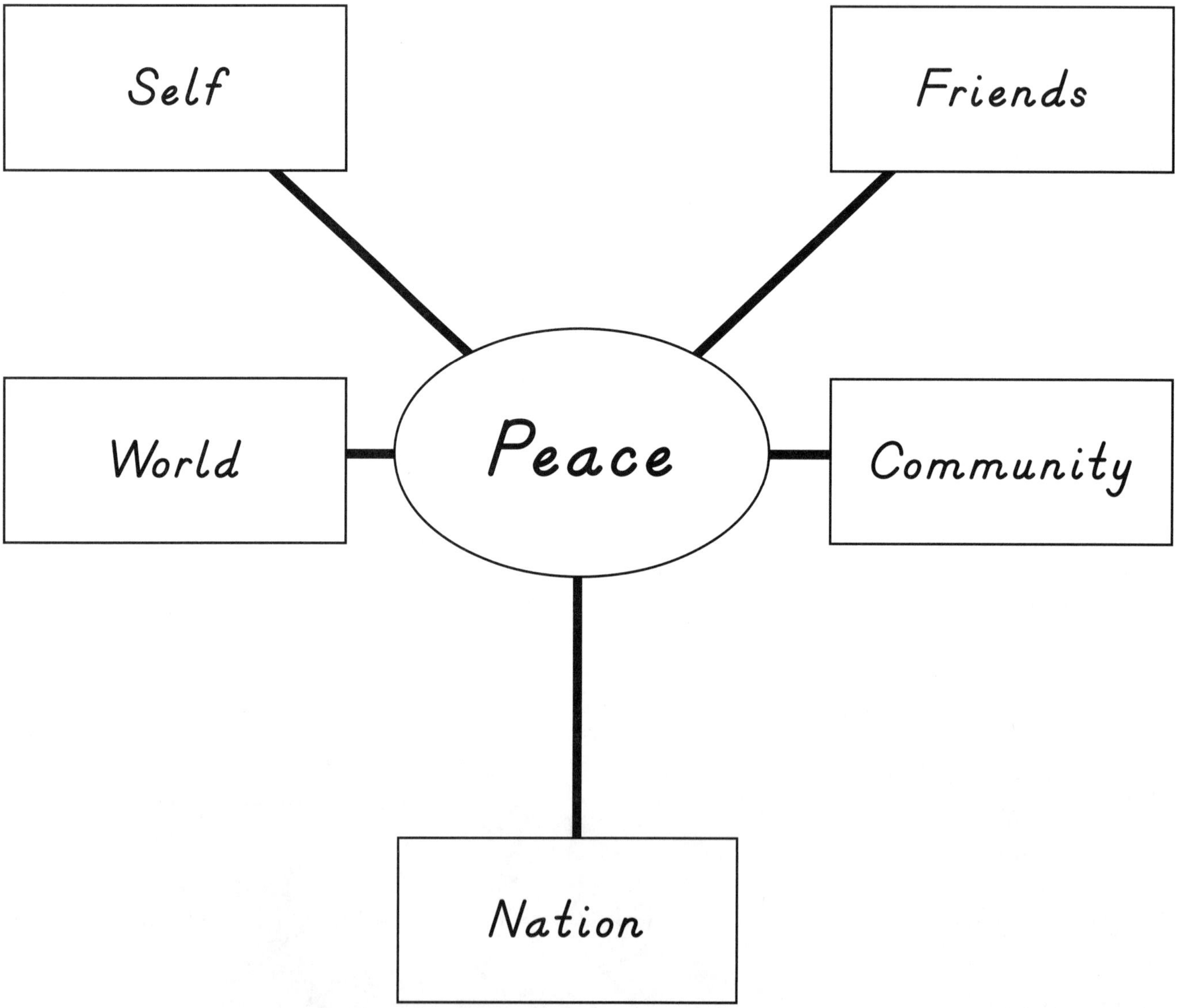

Self

Friends

World

Peace

Community

Nation

◆ Do this cluster on the board with your students.

◆ Discuss each topic. Elicit student definitions of peace at each of these levels.

◆ Discuss the ways in which the different levels are interrelated and the effects that they have on each other.

◆ Ask for suggestions about having peace within oneself, with friends, within a community and a nation, and in the world.

◆ Ask the students to write a paragraph discussing the reasons it is important to begin with themselves in working toward peace. Put these paragraphs away to be compared with the students' views at the conclusion of the unit.

Overview of Activities *(cont.)*

Enjoying the First Book: *Peace Begins with You*

Show the book cover to the class. Discuss the symbolic meaning of the doves. Ask the students to comment on the children in the picture. What are they doing? How do you think the children feel? How do the doves feel about the children? What makes you think so?

Read the title of the book to the class. Ask how it relates to the cluster you did on the board and to the paragraphs they wrote.

Explain to the students that cover flaps sometimes give brief summaries about books. Read the front cover flap of this book to the students and encourage them to comment on the information.

Turn to the back book cover flap and read the students the information about the author and the illustrator. Discuss the function of an illustrator.

Read the book to the class, stopping to show them each of the illustrations. End with a careful reading of "How to be a peacemaker" on the last page of the book.

Reread the book, pausing for discussion of each topic as it is introduced.

Perform *Peace Begins With You* in a readers' theater format. Allow the students time to rehearse. Be ready to present your performance to another classroom or at a school assembly.

Have your students work in a reading response journal over a period of several days as time permits (see pages 200 and 201).

Extending the First Book: *Peace Begins With You*

Have a brainstorming session with the students in which they give their ideas for developing strategies to deal with arguments, teasing, hurt feelings, etc., in the classroom and on the playground. Ask them to choose a few of the ideas they have generated. Write these ideas on a piece of poster paper and display it in the classroom. Encourage your students to try out the ideas and to report on their results. Modify them as needed.

Divide the class into groups. Have each group research a different war, concentrating on the results of that war. Was anything achieved? Did the world become any better? Could the same results have been achieved without a war? If you had been in charge, what would you have done?

Have the students go to the library and research one of these topics:

◆ League of Nations	◆ Berlin Wall
◆ United Nations	◆ Peace Corps
◆ Marshall Plan	◆ NATO
◆ Cold War	◆ OAS

Overview of Activities *(cont.)*

Have your students use pictures from magazines to make collages and/or posters based on one of these slogans: "War is dangerous for children and other living things." "What if they gave a war and nobody came?" or "One nuclear bomb can ruin your whole day."

Ask the students to create their own peace slogans with or without posters. Display them in your classroom.

Have the students collect current event stories centered around peacemaking from their daily newspapers. Discuss the idea that there are more stories about the bad things happening in the world than there are about the good things. Discuss the idea that good things are not usually considered news. Why is this so?

Introduce and discuss the term *compromise*. Did any of the students' ideas for peacekeeping in the classroom or on the playground embody this idea? Which ones? How have they been working in practice?

Have one or more copies of the book available for the class.

Enjoying the Second Book: *The Big Book for Peace*

Show the book cover to the class. Ask if any of the students recognize the illustration. (It is a Maurice Sendak "Wild Thing.") What does the picture symbolize? What is the feeling of the picture?

Read the text on the front and back flaps of the book cover to the students. Discuss the idea that this is a different kind of book from *Peace Begins with You,* but in its own way, it also deals with many different kinds of peace. On the back flap, we are told that the authors and illustrators of this book have donated their royalties to organizations that work for peace. Does this make them peacemakers? Discuss.

Read the statement "How This Book Came to Be" on pages 116 and 117. The people who came up with the idea for this book evidently believe that what people read influences how they think and what they do. Ask the students if they agree with this. Discuss.

Page through the book with the students, displaying and discussing the illustrations. Talk about the different styles and subjects and the differences between fantasy and realism as shown in the artists' treatments of the subject.

Read a story or two aloud to the students.

Have your students continue to work in a reading response journal over a period of several days as time permits (see pages 200 and 201).

Extending the Second Book: *The Big Book for Peace*

After you have read all of the stories aloud to the students, ask them to each choose another book written by one of the authors represented in *The Big Book for Peace.* Have the students read these books independently and report on them to the class. Each student should choose an original way of reporting on his or her book. Some suggestions might be a short talk using props, a poster advertising the book, a play based on the book and involving the help of other students, or a puppet show. (A list of books by these authors follows on pages 195–197.)

Overview of Activities (cont.)

Extending the Second Book: *The Big Book for Peace* (cont.)

Other books by the authors

Lloyd Alexander

The Beggar Queen
Black Cauldron
The Book of Three
Castle of Lly
The Cat Who Wished to Be a Man
The First Two Lives of Lukas-Kasha
The High King
The Kestrel
Marvelous Misadventures of Sebastian
Taran Wanderer
Time Cat
The Town Cats and Other Tales
Westmark
The Wizard in the Tree

Natalie Babbitt

The Devil's Storybook
The Eyes of the Amaryllis
Goody Hall
Herbert Rowbarge
Knee-Knock Rise
Phoebe's Revolt
The Search for Delicious
The Something
Tuck Everlasting

John Bierhorst

The Hungry Woman: Myths and Legends of the Aztecs
The Monkey's Haircut
The Mythology of North America
The Ring in the Prairie
The Sacred Path: Spells, Prayers, and Power Songs of the American Indian

Jean Fritz

And Then What Happened, Paul Revere?
Brady
Brendan the Navigator
The Cabin Faced West
Can't You Make Them Behave, King George?

China Homecoming
The Double Life of Pocahontas
Early Thunder
George Washington's Breakfast

Jean Craighead George

The Cry of the Crow
The Grizzly Bear with the Golden Ears
Hook and Fish, Catch a Mountain
Julie of the Wolves
My Side of the Mountain
One Day in the Alpine Tundra
One Day in the Desert
River Rats
The Summer of the Falcon
The Talking Earth
Who Really Killed Cock Robin?
The Wild, Wild Cookbook: A Guide for Young Wild Food Foragers
The Wounded Wolf

Thacher Hurd

Axle the Freeway Cat
Hobo Dog
Mama Don't Allow
Mystery on the Docks

Steven Kellogg

Can I Keep Him?
Chicken Little
The Island of the Skog
Much Bigger Than Martin
The Mysterious Tadpole
Mystery Beast of Ostergeest
The Mystery of the Flying Orange Pumpkin
The Mystery of the Magic Green Ball
The Mystery of the Missing Red Mitten
The Mystery of the Stolen Blue Paint
The Orchard Cat
Pinkerton, Behave!

Overview of Activities (cont.)

Extending the Second Book: *The Big Book for Peace* (cont.)

Steven Kellogg (cont.)

Ralph's Secret Weapon
A Rose for Pinkerton
Tallyho, Pinkerton!
Won't Somebody Play with Me?

Myra Cohn Livingston

*O Frabjous Day: Poetry for Holidays and
Special Occasions*
Poems of Christmas
Thanksgiving Poems
*Why Am I Grown So Cold: Poems of the
Unknowable*

Lois Lowry

Anastasia Again!
Anastasia, Ask Your Analyst
Anastasia at Your Service
Anastasia Krupnik
Anastasia on Her Own
Autumn Street
Find a Stranger, Say Good-Bye
The One Hundredth Thing About Caroline
A Summer to Die
Switcharound
Taking Care of Terrific
Us and Uncle Fraud

Milton Meltzer

*Ain't Gonna Study War No More: The Story of
America's Peace Seekers*
*All Times, All Peoples: A World History of
Slavery*
Betty Friedan: A Voice for Women's Rights
*The Black Americans: A History in Their Own
Words*
A Book About Names
*Bread and Roses: The Struggle of American
Labor*
Brother, Can You Spare a Dime?
The Chinese Americans
Dorothea Lange: Life Through the Camera
The Hispanic Americans

The Human Rights Book
*In Their Own Words: A History of the
American Negro*
*The Jewish Americans: A History in Their
Own Words*
Langston Hughes: A Biography
Mark Twain
Never to Forget: The Jews of the Holocaust
Poverty
The Right to Remain Silent
Taking Root: Jewish Immigrants in America
The Terrorists
*World of Our Fathers: The Jews of Eastern
Europe*

Katherine Paterson

*Angels and Other Strangers: Family Christmas
Stories*
Bridge to Terabithia
Come Sing, Jimmy Jo
The Great Gilly Hopkins
Jacob Have I Loved
The Master Puppeteer
Of Nightingales That Weep
Rebels of the Heavenly Kingdom
The Sign of the Chrysanthemum

Marilyn Sachs

Amy and Laura
Amy Moves In
Baby Sister
Beach Towels
Bear's House
Bus Ride
Call Me Ruth
Class Pictures
Dorrie's Book
The Fat Girl
Fourteen
Hello. . . Wrong Number
Laura's Luck

Overview of Activities (cont.)

Extending the Second Book: *The Big Book for Peace* (cont.)

Marilyn Sachs (cont.)

A Pocketful of Seeds
A Secret Friend
A Summer's Lease
Thunderbird
Underdog

Maurice Sendak

Alligators All Around
Chicken Soup with Rice
Hector Protector
Higglety Pigglety Pop
In the Night Kitchen
Seven Little Monsters
Very Far Away
Where the Wild Things Are

Yoshiko Uchida

The Best Bad Thing
The Happiest Ending
A Jar of Dreams
Journey Home
Journey to Topaz
The Magic Listening Cap
Samurai of Gold Hill

Mildred Pitts Walter

Because We Are
Brother to the Wind
The Girl on the Outside
My Mama Needs Me
Trouble's Child

Nancy Willard

The Highest Hit
The Island of the Grass King
The Marzipan Moon
The Nightgown of the Sullen Moon
Papa's Panda
Sailing to Cythera
Simple Pictures Are Best
Stranger's Bread
Uncle Terrible: More Adventures of Anatole

Charlotte Zolotow

The Beautiful Christmas Tree
Big Brother
Big Sister and Little Sister
The Bunny Who Found Easter
But Not Billy
Do You Know What I'll Do?
A Father Like That
Flocks of Birds
The Hating Book
Hold My Hand
I Have a Horse of My Own
I Know a Lady
If It Weren't for You
If You Listen
It's Not Fair
Janey
May I Visit?
Mr. Rabbit and the Lovely Present
My Friend John
My Grandson Lew
The New Friend
One Step, Two . . .
Over and Over
Park Book
The Quarreling Book
River Winding
Say It!
The Sky Was Blue
Some Things Go Together
Someday
Someone New
The Song
Storm Book

(Works by the illustrators can be found in *Children's Books in Print*, R.R. Bowker Co., New York and London.)

Writing Topics

1. Read the Introduction for *The Big Book for Peace* aloud to the students. In it the editors say, "We hope that you will write your own stories and poems about peace, draw your own pictures, and sing your own songs." Remind the students of the variety of the stories that are included in *The Big Book for Peace*—some fact, some fantasy, some serious, some funny.

   Have each student write his or her own peace story and/or poem and illustrate it, if desired. Students who do not wish to illustrate their own stories could have one of the "class artists" read and illustrate it. Point out to the students that most writers do not illustrate their own books, although there are notable exceptions such as Maurice Sendak and Thacher Hurd.

   If you use the writing process, allow the stories and poems to go through the complete process— rough draft, self-editing, peer editing, revision, and so on—until the students are pleased with the products. Then allow the students to make final copies, either by hand or by using the word processor. (If you are lucky, you may have the option of doing this whole process on a computer.) Have your students complete their illustrations.

   Bind the compiled results and celebrate your published peace book. If possible, make multiple copies and then present at least one to your school library. Have a presentation ceremony and invite the principal and the parents.

2. Write peace songs as a whole class, in groups, or individually. Play some peace songs to motivate the students and give them some ideas. Some notable songs that have been recorded by a number of different artists are "We Are the World," "Give Peace a Chance," "Let There Be Peace on Earth," and "Blowin' in the Wind."

3. The last page of *Peace Begins with You* is entitled "How to be a peacemaker." Have a student volunteer read this page aloud to the class. Then divide the class into groups and ask each group to make up its own list of things to do to be peacemakers. Compare and discuss the completed lists. Either compile them into one list or post the group lists for the students to read and appreciate.

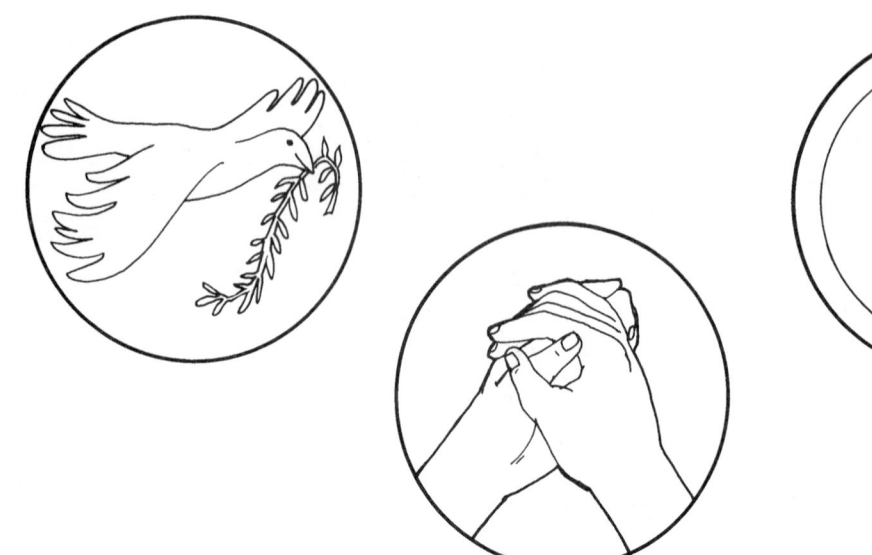

Writing Topics *(cont.)*

4. Write a letter to one or all of the peace organizations listed in *The Big Book for Peace*. Ask them for information that would be suitable for your classroom and for posters and any other materials they might want to send you.

   Note: It would be wise to review this material before sharing it with your class. Some of the material about war may be much too graphic for your students. The Lion and the Lamb Peace Arts Center may have materials which are the most directly prepared for children.

   Amnesty International

   322 Eighth Avenue

   New York, NY 10001

   The Carter Center Peace Fund

   P.O. Box 105515

   Atlanta, GA 30307

   Greenpeace

   1436 U Street, N.W.

   Washington, D.C. 20009

   The Lion and the Lamb Peace Arts Center

   Bluffton College

   Bluffton, OH 45817

   SANE/FREEZE: Campaign for Global Security

   711 G St., S.E.

   Washington, D.C. 20003

5. Ask the students to write paragraphs discussing the reasons which make it important to begin with themselves in working toward peace. Compare these paragraphs with those written on the same subject at the beginning of the unit. Discuss.

Reading Response Journals

Peace Begins With You

Reading response journals are a good technique to use in helping students make the connection between what they read and how they feel. This encourages the higher order thinking skills of analysis, synthesis, and evaluation.

Have your students divide their notebook pages into two columns and label them as shown below.

Quotation From Story	*My Response*

Have each student copy a quotation from the list below in the left-hand column of his or her notebook. Tell them to then write their responses to the quotations in their right-hand columns.

Quotations

1. "Peace can feel warm, bright, and strong—or calm, cool, and gentle."

2. "Peace means different things to different people, in different places, at different times in their lives."

3. "Peace is being allowed to be different—and letting others be different from you."

4. "So what can be done when people's needs or wants don't seem to fit together?"

5. "Conflict can be the beginning of something new, and good."

6. "There are always choices that can be made."

7. "Some choices threaten peace. Some choices protect it."

8. "Working for peace may be harder than using force."

9. "Our world is full of change."

10. "Peace is not a gap between times of fighting, or a space where nothing is happening."

11. "Peace is something that lives, grows, spreads—and needs to be looked after."

Reading Response Journals *(cont.)*

The Big Book for Peace

Continue the process that was begun for *Peace Begins with You.*

Have your students turn to a new notebook page and divide it into two columns as before.

Quotation From Story	My Response

Have each student copy a quotation from the list below in the left-hand column of his or her notebook. Tell them to then write their responses to the quotations in their right-hand columns.

The quotations below are selections from a variety of stories in the book. Students may want to look back over the story from which a quotation is taken in order to remember the context. You may also wish to add other quotations that you feel are meaningful or select statements from stories that your class liked the best.

Quotations

1. "If everyone has the same dream, it might come true."

   —from "The Dream" by Steven Kellogg

2. "At a time like this, one could believe that anything was possible."

   —from "There Is an Island" by Jean Fritz

3. "What other game is there to play?"

   —from "The Game" by Myra Cohn Livingston

4. 'The very best part,' she said finally, 'is the bridge.'

   —from "The Tree House" by Lois Lowry

5. 'There can be no peace without freedom,' Papa said.

   'And you think someone is going to give you freedom?' Mama asked with heat in her voice. 'Instead of going to Washington, you should be getting a gun to protect us.'

   'There are ways to win a struggle without bombs and guns. I'm going to Washington and Craig is going with me.'

   —from "The Silent Lobby" by Mildred Pitts Walter

Across the Curriculum

Art

1. Create anti-war slogans and posters. These can consist of collages made up of pictures cut from magazines or newspapers or original designs done in poster paint.

2. Make original illustrations. Have the students each choose one of the books they read together or individually and make new illustrations for it. Use the student-made illustrations together with the books they are based on for a classroom display.

3. Have each child create a symbol of what peace means to him or her. Display the symbols on a bulletin board with the title "Peace Is . . . ."

4. Experiment with watercolors. Let the students paint non-representational impressions of what peace feels like. Play music during this art experience. (Beethoven's "Ode to Joy" makes for a nice experience.)

Music

1. If you wrote peace songs either as a whole class, group, or as individuals, set them to music. (See Writing Topics, Activity 2, page 198.) Make up your own tunes or use familiar tunes that everyone knows.

2. Get the sheet music for a song like "Let There Be Peace on Earth" and learn to sing it as a class.

3. Make a habit of playing music as background for quiet work times. Vary the types and tempos of music. Discuss the effect this has with the students.

Language Arts

1. Create vocabulary exercises and word search activities based on the reading vocabulary. (See page 206 for a sample activity.)

2. Make up language activities with a "Peaceful Parts of Speech" theme. (See page 207 for a sample.)

3. Create your weekly lists of spelling words for tests, using words from the students' reading and writing activities.

4. Have your students pretend that they are running for office on the "Peace Platform." They should each prepare a three-minute campaign speech to persuade other class members to vote for them. Stage a mock election based on the speeches.

Across the Curriculum *(cont.)*

Social Science

1. Keep the classroom world map pulled down and refer to it routinely in discussing both current and past events associated with war and peace.

2. Encourage your students to find the places that are being discussed on the globe as well as on the map.

3. Help your students who are doing research to turn the statistics they come across into graphic representations (line, bar, and circle graphs, as well as charts). This manner of presenting facts will appeal to the visual learners and will also help all of the students to learn a valuable skill.

4. Challenge your students to explore world history to find a time when there were no wars in the world. Let them check one another's information.

Science

1. Many people feel that solving the problem of world hunger will be a big step toward world peace. Have the students do research to find out the branches of science that are working on this problem. If possible, invite a scientist from a college or other establishment near you to come and talk to your class about developments in this field.

2. The science of ecology is closely related to world peace. How can the scientists who want to save the environments and the people who feel that they need to use natural resources settle their differences peacefully? Help your students to become aware of this problem by presenting material from both points of view in a problem solving situation. (For example, the native people in the Amazon are cutting down or burning parts of the rain forests in order to raise food crops.)

3. The disposal of wastes and the prevention of pollution are other areas that concern ecologists. Ask students to do some research to find out how these problems could have an effect on world peace. Discuss. (For example, many United States firms have moved their factories over the border into Mexico to escape the laws that regulate pollution and waste disposal.)

Across the Curriculum *(cont.)*

Math

1. Almost any kind of a word problem can be stated in terms having to do with peace. For example, if there has been a war somewhere in the world during 80 of the past 100 years, for what percentage of that century has the world been at peace?

2. All of the graphing skills that were mentioned in the "Social Science" section are practical applications of math.

Life Skills

Careers:

Brainstorm with your students to discover possible careers that would be compatible with being a peacemaker. Have them do some research to discover other possible career paths in this area.

Investigate the career backgrounds of people who have become associated with the peace movement in one way or another. Encourage your students to share their information with the class.

Some people to investigate might include the following:

Eleanor Roosevelt	Dag Hammarskjöld	Martin Luther King, Jr.
Mother Teresa	Desmond Tutu	Peter Ueberroth
Ralph Bunche	Mahatma Gandhi	

Physical Education

Investigate Akido for ideas for some non-competitive games and activities. There are many activities associated with Akido that have been developed to help children build skills in cooperation and non-violence.

Cooking

Invite someone to come to your school to demonstrate a solar cooker. These devices are being used in many third world countries with great success. Contact a representative of the Peace Corps as a possible source of this information.

Discuss with the students the advantages of solar cookers (e.g., free fuel) and the disadvantages (e.g., they only work when the sun is shining).

Culminating Activities

Peace Party

This unit should culminate in an appropriate celebration such as a classroom party to which parents and administrators could be invited. Several of the activities imbedded in the unit could be presented to this audience, making it unnecessary to prepare any new material.

1. The presentation of the students' Peace Book (see "Writing Topics," page 198) could be done at this time. If the book has already been presented to the school library, a student could display the book and tell about the presentation. Copies of the book should be available for party guests to enjoy.

2. If the class has written or learned a peace song, it could be performed as part of the unit culmination. Make copies of the lyrics and ask the guests to join in.

3. This would be the perfect time to present the readers' theater performance of *Peace Begins With You*. (See "Enjoying the First Book," page 193.)

4. Assemble and display all of the artwork, posters, slogans, journals, graphs, and charts that have been produced during the development of the unit. You can also display the assortment of books that you have accumulated and read, together with any material obtained by writing to peace organizations.

5. Make an effort to find someone to videotape your party. It will be a perfect addition to your open house display at the end of the year.

6. Use the peace party invitation below to invite guests to your party.

Peace Word Search

On a separate piece of paper, write a short definition of each of these words. Then find the words in the word search.

arguments	enemy	peacemaker
changes	fighting	problems
choices	friend	solutions
differences	needs	wants
doves	peace	war

```
W  R  C  G  Q  O  P  B  C  F  H  P  V  E  W  D  A  X  Z  E  R
N  C  A  Q  N  R  T  Y  U  H  G  E  S  N  A  I  Q  D  T  I  C
C  F  T  E  R  P  E  A  C  E  M  A  K  E  R  F  S  E  R  T  Y
G  R  C  D  E  O  P  R  U  Y  P  C  M  M  N  F  A  Q  W  S  D
P  L  M  N  D  I  K  G  H  N  R  E  R  Y  L  E  S  W  E  R  T
L  K  J  H  S  O  L  U  T  I  O  N  S  O  I  R  I  U  Y  T  R
M  N  B  V  C  X  F  M  W  E  B  I  R  Y  T  E  E  W  Q  A  S
W  D  V  G  F  R  I  E  N  D  L  Q  C  E  R  N  S  D  G  H  J
G  F  E  W  Q  A  G  N  V  C  E  C  H  O  I  C  E  S  S  D  F
G  T  F  C  S  X  H  T  R  T  M  N  A  U  J  E  Z  S  D  F  G
P  L  M  Q  A  N  T  S  J  H  S  O  N  P  L  S  L  K  J  H  G
O  I  U  A  U  Y  I  M  N  B  V  C  G  F  G  Y  U  J  K  O  P
Z  X  E  B  T  Y  N  I  U  D  O  V  E  S  U  U  T  R  E  W  Q
A  S  D  F  G  H  F  Q  W  E  R  T  S  A  S  D  F  G  H  J  K
```

Peaceful Parts of Speech

Teacher's Note: Ask your students for the parts of speech listed under the blanks and then insert the words. Read the completed story or have a student volunteer to read it aloud.

One_____I decided to_____ for peace.
　　　　　(noun)　　　　　　　　　　　　　　　　*(verb)*

I made myself a_____sign and joined a peace
　　　　　　　　　　　(adjective)

demonstration. My friend and_____were happy to be a
　　　　　　　　　　　　　　　　(pronoun)

part of such a dedicated_____, and we marched
　　　　　　　　　　　　　　　(noun)

_____down the street,
　　　　　　　　(adverb)

_____our signs in the_____.
　　　("ing" verb)　　　　　　　　　　　*(noun)*

_____! It was a long day_____a
　　　(interjection)　　　　　　　　　　　　*(conjunction)*

different_____. We met many_____and
　　　　　(noun)　　　　　　　　　　　　　*(plural noun)*

made some_____ _____.
　　　　　(adjective)　　　　　　　*(plural noun)*

The next day_____were_____but we
　　　　　　　　(pronoun)　　　　　　　*(adjective)*

were _____ _____.
　　　(adverb)　　　　　　　　*(adjective)*

Resources and References

CCRC (Children's Creative Response to Conflict)

P.O. Box 271

Nyack, NY 10960

(914) 358-4601

Children's Creative Response to Conflict presents many kinds of teacher training programs throughout the United States. As an extension of their standard workshops and courses, they will custom-design workshops to meet a group's time and theme requirements. Their handbook, *The Friendly Classroom for a Small Planet* by Priscilla Prutzman et al., is a wonderful resource. In addition to many creative lesson plans and ideas, it lists dozens of regional CCRC branches and related programs. Also available are a newsletter, *Sharing Space*, and a literature service featuring books, articles, and a slide show on the CCRC program.

Sunburst Communications

101 Castleton Street

P.O. Box 40

Pleasantville, NY 10570-9807

Phone: 1-800-431-1934

FAX: (914) 769-2109

Sunburst Communications offers videos, games, newsletters, and posters for grades K–12 on various subjects of guidance and health. They offer several videos specifically on conflict resolution. Request a catalog for more details about their products.

❖ Canter, Lee and Katia Petersen. *Teaching Students to Get Along.* Lee Canter and Associates, 1995.

❖ Faber, Adele and Elaine Mazlish. *How to Talk so Kids Can Learn: At Home and in School.* Rawson Associates, 1995.

❖ Gardner, Howard. *Frames of Mind: The Theory of Multiple Intelligences.* Basic Books, 1983.

❖ Porro, Barbara. *Talk It Out: Conflict Resolution in the Elementary Classroom.* Association for Supervision and Curriculum Development, 1996.

❖ Prutzman, Priscilla et al. *The Friendly Classroom for a Small Planet: A Handbook on Creative Approaches to Living and Problem Solving.* New Society Publishers, 1988.